Bake Sale Bestsellers

for Funds and Friendship

Cindy Baker

Published by Cookbook Resources, LLC

Bake Sale Bestsellers

1st Printing September 2005

ISBN 1-931294-40-2

Library of Congress Number: 2005933062

Illustrated by Nancy Bohanan
Edited, Designed and Published in the
United States of America and
Manufactured in China by
Cookbook Resources, LLC
541 Doubletree Drive
Highland Village, Texas 75077
Toll free 866-229-2665
www.cookbookresources.com

Table of Contents

Introduction

Bake sales have long been favorite ways of raising funds for schools, religious organizations and social clubs. With neither overhead nor capital, bake sales are great moneymakers for a group with a project in focus, a charity with a cause, or a mission with a goal. And bake sales are popular because they become social events at which people mix, mingle and enjoy the satisfaction of working together for a common purpose. The success of a bake sale depends on the clear recipe of the intended goal, the ingredients of the organization, and the temperature of the market. Here are some tips for a purposeful and profitable bake sale where the "ize" have it.

Strategize

- Plan a bake sale around a festive holiday when people are buying.
- Decide on a worthwhile goal for the fundraiser.
- Target women—they'll buy weeks' worth of goodies to freeze for later.
- Select a high-traffic area, like a sporting event or a theater production.
- Take orders in advance.
- Pass out sign-up sheets to your group to ensure a variety of baked goods.
- Stage a 2-day baking marathon in a local church, school, etc.

Advertise

- Design a flyer and distribute to neighborhoods, stores, and schools.
- Send a sample box of goodies along with the flyer to radio or TV stations.
- Find a business that will match or double your sales.
- Promote by email—it's free!
- Provide free delivery to those who can't make it to the sale.

Glamorize

- Decorate the bake sale area with your organization's or the holiday's colors.
- Use tablecloths that enhance the baked goods, not overpower them.
- Cover the baked goods with clear wrap and dress up with ribbons, etc.
- Label the item—mystery foods don't sell.
- Include the recipe.
- Tuck a thank-you card inside each baked item.
- Make it a social event with live music, cooking or craft demonstrations, etc.

Merchandize

- Prominently display the name of the organization and fund raising purpose.
- Establish a variety of prices.
- Go for simplicity by pricing in increments of 25 cents.
- Bring a cash box with change, price stickers and marking pens.
- Offer a sample plate of tiny pieces of baked goods and small cups of water.
- Appeal to children and seniors by offering single-serving selections.
- Place individual cookie sales in a large glass cookie jar.
- Buy serving platters at flea markets to be included with baked displays.
- Arrange tables by categories, i.e., cakes, pies, candies, cookies, etc.
- Make extra money—sell fresh-brewed coffee, lemonade, or bottled water.
- If location permits, bake on the premises—the aroma will cinch the sale.
- Create goodie baskets that can be purchased as gifts.
- Furnish large bags to encourage multiple purchases.
- Raffle off distinctive creations.
- Should sales become slow, conduct hourly specials.

Chocolate-Praline Layer Cake

$^1/_2$ cup (1 stick) butter
$^1/_4$ cup whipping cream
1 cup packed brown sugar
1 cup chopped pecans, divided
1 18 oz. box devil's food cake mix with
  pudding
1$^1/_4$ cups water
1 cup oil
3 eggs

- In small saucepan, combine butter, whipping cream and brown sugar. Cook over low heat until butter melts and stir occasionally.

- Pour butter mixture into two lightly greased 8 or 9-inch cake pans and sprinkle each with $^1/_2$ cup pecans.

- In large bowl, combine cake mix, water, oil and eggs with mixer at low speed until moistened and beat two minutes at highest speed. Spoon batter over pecan mixture.

- Bake at 350° for 35 to 45 minutes or until cake springs back when touched lightly in center. Cool in pans for only 5 minutes. Remove from pans and cool completely.

- Place one layer on serving plate with praline side up. Top with second layer also with praline side up. Garnish with dollops of whipped cream, chocolate curls and pecans if desired.

Milky Way Cake

8 (2 ounce) Milky Way candy bars
1 cup (2 sticks) butter, $\frac{1}{2}$ cup melted,
  $\frac{1}{2}$ cup softened
1$\frac{1}{2}$ cups sugar
4 eggs, separated
1 teaspoon vanilla extract
1$\frac{1}{2}$ cups buttermilk
1 teaspoon baking soda
3 cups flour
1 cup chopped pecans

- Combine candy bars and $\frac{1}{2}$ cup (1 stick) melted butter in saucepan and place over low heat until bars melt. Cool.
- Cream $\frac{1}{2}$ cup (1 stick) softened butter and sugar.
- Add egg yolks one at a time and beat well after each addition. Stir in vanilla.
- Combine buttermilk and baking soda. Add buttermilk mixture to creamed mixture alternately with flour and beat well.
- Stir in candy mixture and pecans and fold in stiffly beaten egg whites.
- Pour batter into greased bundt pan.
- Bake at 325° for 35 minutes.

Super Strawberry Cake

1 (18 ounce) box white cake mix
4 eggs
1 cup oil
$\frac{1}{2}$ cup water
1 (3 ounce) box strawberry gelatin mix
Juice from thawed strawberries

- Combine all cake ingredients and blend thoroughly with mixer.
- Pour into two greased 9-inch cake pans.
- Bake at 350° for 35 minutes.

Frosting:
$\frac{1}{4}$ cup ($\frac{1}{2}$ stick) butter
1 (16 ounce) carton frozen, sweetened strawberries, thawed
1 (16 ounce) box powdered sugar

- Combine all frosting ingredients and beat with mixer until thoroughly blended.
- Spread on cooled Super Strawberry Cake.

Plum Good Cake

2 cups self-rising flour
2 cups sugar
1 cup oil
3 eggs
2 (2.5 ounce) jars plum baby food
1 teaspoon cinnamon
1 teaspoon cloves

- Combine flour, sugar, oil, eggs, baby food, cinnamon and cloves in mixing bowl and beat for 3 minutes.
- Pour into greased tube or bundt pan.
- Bake at 325° for 1 hour.

Glaze:
1 (16 ounce) box powdered sugar
$^1/_4$ cup milk
1 tablespoon lemon juice

- Mix all glaze ingredients and drizzle mixture over warm cake.

Raspberry-Fudge Cake

1 cup flour
$^3/_4$ teaspoon baking powder
$^1/_4$ teaspoon salt
4 (1 ounce) squares semi-sweet baking
  chocolate, divided
4 (1 ounce) squares unsweetened baking
  chocolate
$^3/_4$ cup (1$^1/_2$ sticks) plus 1 tablespoon butter
$^3/_4$ cup sugar
1 cup seedless raspberry jam, divided
$^1/_4$ cup cherry liqueur or maraschino cherry
  juice
3 eggs

- Sift flour, baking powder and salt and set aside.

- Melt 3 semi-sweet chocolate squares, unsweetened chocolate squares and $^3/_4$ cup butter in heavy saucepan over low heat and stir constantly.

- Whisk sugar, $^3/_4$ cup jam, liqueur and eggs in large bowl. Whisk in chocolate mixture and flour mixture.

(Continued on next page.)

(Continued)

- Pour into greased 9-inch springform pan dusted with cocoa.
- Bake at 350° for 40 to 45 minutes or until set. Cool on wire rack 10 minutes.
- Remove sides of pan and cool completely on wire rack.
- Melt remaining semi-sweet chocolate square and 1 tablespoon butter in heavy saucepan over low heat and stir constantly.
- Spread remaining $1/4$ cup jam over top of cake and drizzle with chocolate mixture.

Apricot-Almond Upside-Down Cake

¹/₄ cup (¹/₂ stick) butter, melted
1 (16 ounce) can apricot halves, drained
¹/₃ cup packed brown sugar
¹/₃ cup sliced almonds
1 (16 ounce) package pound cake mix
1 teaspoon vanilla extract
1 teaspoon almond extract

- Pour butter into 9-inch round cake pan.
- Place apricot halves, cut side up, in pan and sprinkle with brown sugar and almonds.
- Prepare pound cake batter according to package directions and stir in extracts.
- Pour batter over apricot halves.
- Bake at 350° for 35 minutes or until toothpick inserted in center comes out clean.
- Run knife around edge of cake to loosen and invert onto serving plate.

Five-Flavor Pound Cake

1 cup (2 sticks) butter
$\frac{1}{2}$ cup oil
3 cups sugar
5 eggs, beaten
3 cups flour
1 teaspoon baking powder
1 cup milk
1 teaspoon each vanilla, rum, butter, coconut and lemon extracts

- Cream butter, oil and sugar until light and add eggs one at a time. Cream until fluffy.
- Mix flour and baking powder and add to creamed mixture alternately with milk.
- Stir in extracts.
- Pour batter into greased tube or bundt pan.
- Bake at 325° for 1 hour 30 minutes or until cake tests done.

13

Tater-Mocha Pound Cake

1 tablespoon instant coffee granules
2 tablespoons hot water
1½ cups low-fat milk
2 cups flour
2 cups sugar
1 cup instant potato flakes
4 teaspoons baking powder
½ teaspoon salt
1 (3.9 ounce) package instant chocolate
  pudding mix
1 cup (2 sticks) butter
4 eggs

- Combine coffee granules and hot water in small bowl and stir until coffee dissolves. Stir in milk.

- Combine flour, sugar, potato flakes, baking powder, salt, pudding mix, butter and eggs in large mixing bowl. Beat at low speed until batter mixes.

- Beat in coffee mixture and continue to beat at medium speed for 4 minutes.

- Scrape batter into greased bundt pan.

- Bake at 350° for 55 minutes or until toothpick inserted near center comes out clean. Cool in pan for 30 minutes.

Chocolate Chip Pound Cake

1 (18 ounce) box yellow cake mix
4 eggs
$\frac{1}{2}$ cup oil
1 (6 ounce) package chocolate chips
1 (3.4 ounce) package instant vanilla
pudding mix
1 (8 ounce) carton sour cream
1 (4 ounce) package German sweet baking
chocolate, grated
1 cup chopped pecans

- Mix cake mix, eggs, oil, $\frac{1}{2}$ cup water, chocolate chips and pudding mix and whisk until smooth.
- Add sour cream, baking chocolate and pecans and mix. Pour into greased bundt or tube pan.
- Bake at 325° for 55 minutes. Remove from pan.

Tip: Cake is good plain or with Cream Cheese Frosting. (See page 18.)

Old-Fashioned Pound Cake

1 cup (2 sticks) butter, softened
1/3 cup shortening
5 eggs, room temperature
3 cups sugar
3 cups flour
1/2 teaspoon baking powder
1/2 teaspoon baking soda
1/2 teaspoon salt
1 (8 ounce) carton sour cream
2 teaspoons vanilla extract
1 teaspoon coconut flavoring

- Cream butter and shortening, add sugar and cream well.

- Add eggs one at a time and beat well after each addition. Add vanilla and coconut flavoring.

- Sift flour, baking powder, baking soda and salt. Add flour mixture to batter a little at a time alternating with sour cream. Pour batter into greased bundt pan.

- Bake at 350° for 1 hour. Remove from oven and cool 10 minutes.

German Chocolate Pound Cake

2 cups sugar
1 cup shortening
4 eggs, beaten
2 teaspoons vanilla extract
2 teaspoons butter flavoring
3 cups flour
$1/2$ teaspoon baking soda
1 teaspoon salt
1 cup buttermilk
1 (4 ounce) package German sweet baking chocolate, grated

- Cream sugar and shortening. Add eggs, vanilla and butter flavoring and set aside.
- Sift together flour, baking soda and salt.
- Add flour mixture to creamed mixture alternately with buttermilk. (Begin and end with flour mixture.)
- Add German chocolate and place batter in greased bundt pan.
- Bake at 300° for 1 hour 30 minutes.

Squash Cake

3 cups sugar
1 1/2 cups oil
4 eggs
3 cups grated squash
1 cup chopped nuts
2 teaspoons baking powder
1 teaspoon baking soda
1 1/2 teaspoons cinnamon
1/2 teaspoon salt
4 cups flour

- Mix sugar, oil eggs and squash and add nuts, baking powder, baking soda, cinnamon, salt and flour. Pour batter into greased tube pan.
- Bake at 300° for 1 hour 30 minutes.
- When cake is cool, spread with Cream Cheese Frosting (recipe below).

Cream Cheese Frosting:
1 (8 ounce) package cream cheese, softened
1/2 cup (1 stick) butter, softened
1 (16 ounce) box powdered sugar
1 teaspoon vanilla extract

- Beat cream cheese and butter at medium speed until fluffy. Gradually add sugar and beat well. Stir in vanilla.

Pumpkin Pound Cake

2 cups sugar
4 eggs
1¼ cups oil
2 cups flour
1 teaspoon salt
2 teaspoons baking soda
3 teaspoons cinnamon
1 (15 ounce) can pumpkin

- Blend granulated sugar, eggs and oil.
- Sift together flour, salt, baking soda and cinnamon. Add flour mixture to sugar mixture alternately with pumpkin and mix well after each addition.
- Pour batter into greased tube pan.
- Bake at 350° for 1 hour.
  Cool 20 to 25 minutes.

Frosting:
½ cup (1 stick) butter
1 (8 ounce) package cream cheese
1 teaspoon vanilla extract
1 (16 ounce) box powdered sugar
½ cup chopped pecans

- Combine all frosting ingredients and mix until smooth. Spread over cake when it cools completely.

Old-Fashioned Carrot Cake

1 (10 ounce) package shredded carrots
2 cups flour
1 teaspoon baking soda
1 teaspoon baking powder
$1/2$ teaspoon salt
2 cups sugar
1 teaspoon cinnamon
4 eggs, beaten
$3/4$ cup oil
1 teaspoon vanilla extract

- Combine carrots, flour, baking soda, baking powder, salt, sugar and cinnamon in bowl. Add eggs, oil and vanilla and stir until they blend.
- Pour batter into three greased, wax paper-lined 9-inch round cake pans.
- Bake at 350° for 25 minutes or until toothpick inserted in center comes out clean. Cool in pans for 10 minutes. Remove and cool on wire racks.
- Spread Cream Cheese Frosting (see page 18) between layers, and on top and sides of cooled cake.

Kahlua Cake

1 (18 ounce) chocolate cake mix without
 pudding
1 (3.4 ounce) package instant vanilla
 pudding, prepared
1 (6 ounce) package chocolate chips
2 eggs
1 (16 ounce) carton sour cream
$^1/_4$ cup oil
$^1/_3$ cup kahlua

- Combine all ingredients.
- Pour batter into greased bundt pan.
- Bake at 350° for 30 to 45 minutes or until
 toothpick inserted in center of cake comes
 out clean.

Yummy Rum Cake

1 cup chopped pecans or walnuts
1 (18 ounce) box yellow cake mix
1 (3.4 ounce) package instant vanilla
  pudding mix
4 eggs
1/2 cup oil
1/2 cup light or dark rum

- Combine all ingredients except nuts, with 1/4 cup cold water.
- Sprinkle nuts into greased 10-inch tube or bundt pan and pour batter over nuts.
- Bake at 325° for 1 hour. Cool for 30. minutes and invert onto serving plate.

Glaze:
1/2 cup (1 stick) butter
1 cup sugar
1/2 cup rum

- Melt butter in saucepan and stir in 1/4 cup water and sugar.
- Boil for 5 minutes and stir constantly. Remove from heat, cool slightly and stir in rum slowly.
- Prick all over top of cake with toothpick. Drizzle and smooth glaze evenly over top and sides and allow glaze to soak into cake.

Snappy Wine Cake

1 (18 ounce) box yellow cake mix
1 (3.4 ounce) package instant vanilla
  pudding mix
4 eggs
¾ oil
¾ cup sherry
1 teaspoon nutmeg

- Combine all ingredients and beat with mixer
  for about 5 minutes at medium speed.
- Pour batter into greased tube pan.
- Bake at 350° for 45 minutes. Cool in pan
  5 minutes and sprinkle with powdered sugar.

Black Walnut Cake

1 cup (2 sticks) butter
2 cups sugar
2 cups flour
1 cup chopped black walnuts
1 teaspoon lemon extract
1 teaspoon vanilla extract
6 eggs

- Cream butter and sugar on high speed. Add
  flour, walnuts, extracts and eggs gradually
  and mix on high for 5 minutes.
- Pour batter into greased tube or bundt pan.
- Bake at 350° for 50 to 60 minutes.

Red Velvet Cake

$^1/_2$ cup shortening
$1^1/_2$ cups sugar
2 eggs
2 ounces red food coloring
2 tablespoons cocoa
1 scant teaspoon salt
$1^1/_4$ cups flour
1 teaspoon vanilla extract
1 teaspoon baking soda
1 cup buttermilk
1 tablespoon vinegar
1 teaspoon butter flavoring

- Cream shortening, sugar and eggs.
- Make paste of food coloring and cocoa and add to creamed mixture.
- Add salt and flour alternately with buttermilk and vanilla.
- Add baking soda and vinegar. Blend, but do not beat.
- Pour batter into two greased 8-inch round cake pans.
- Bake at 350° for 30 minutes. Frost when cooled.

(Continued on next page.)

 Cakes

(Continued)

Frosting:
3 tablespoons flour
1 cup milk
1 cup sugar
1 cup shortening
1 teaspoon vanilla extract

- Cook flour and milk on low heat until thick. Cool.
- Cream sugar, shortening and vanilla until fluffy and add to flour-milk mixture.
- Beat until mixture is like whipped cream.
- Frost between layers, on sides and over top of cooled cake.

Sponge Cake

5 eggs
1 cup sugar, divided
1½ teaspoons grated lemon rind
1½ teaspoons lemon juice
1 cup flour
¼ teaspoon salt
¼ teaspoon cream of tartar

- Separate egg yolks from egg whites and set whites aside.
- Beat egg yolks and gradually add ½ cup sugar.
- Combine lemon rind, lemon juice and 2 tablespoons water. Gradually add lemon mixture to egg yolks and beat constantly until mixture is very thick and light.
- Add flour all at once and beat until ingredients combine well.
- Beat egg whites and salt until foamy. Add cream of tartar and continue beating until soft peaks form.
- Add remaining ½ cup sugar, 2 tablespoons at a time and beat until stiff but not dry.
- Fold into egg yolk mixture and pour into ungreased tube pan.
- Bake at 375° for 30 minutes.

Fruit-Swirl Coffee Cake

1½ cups sugar
½ cup (1 stick) butter
½ cup shortening
1½ teaspoons baking powder
1 teaspoon vanilla extract
1 teaspoon almond extract
4 eggs
3 cups flour
1 (20 ounce) can cherry pie filling

- Blend sugar, butter, shortening, baking powder, extracts and eggs in large mixing bowl. Beat on low speed and scrape bowl constantly. Beat 3 minutes on high speed and scrape bowl occasionally.

- Stir in flour and spread two-thirds batter in greased jellyroll pan or two greased 9 x 9-inch pans.

- Spread pie filling over batter and drop remaining batter by tablespoonfuls onto pie filling. Bake at 350° for 45 minutes.

Glaze:
1 cup powdered sugar
1 to 2 tablespoons milk

- Combine glaze ingredients and stir until smooth. Drizzle glaze over warm cake.

Applesauce Coffee Cake

1³/₄ cups flour, divided
¹/₂ cup sugar
¹/₂ cup (1 stick) butter
¹/₄ cup chopped nuts
¹/₂ teaspoon cinnamon
1¹/₂ teaspoons baking powder
¹/₂ teaspoon baking soda
2 eggs, beaten
1 cup applesauce or apple butter
1 teaspoon vanilla extract

- Combine ³/₄ cup flour and sugar and cut in butter until mixture is crumbly. Reserve ¹/₂ cup crumb mixture for topping and combine reserved crumbs with nuts and cinnamon. Set aside.
- Add 1 cup flour, baking powder and baking soda to remaining crumb mixture.
- Add eggs, applesauce and vanilla and beat until mixture blends well.
- Pour batter into greased 9 x 9-inch pan and sprinkle reserved crumb mixture over top.
- Bake at 375° for 30 to 35 minutes.

Fresh Apple Coffee Cake

2 tablespoons plus $\frac{1}{2}$ cup sugar
$\frac{1}{2}$ teaspoon salt
2 tablespoons ($\frac{1}{4}$ stick) butter, softened
  divided
1 egg, beaten
$\frac{3}{4}$ cup milk
2 cups plus 2 tablespoons flour
2 teaspoons baking powder
1 teaspoon vanilla extract
5 or 6 apples, peeled, sliced

- Blend 2 tablespoons sugar, salt and
  1 tablespoon butter.
- Add egg and milk and mix well.
- Stir in 2 cups flour, baking powder and
  vanilla and blend well.
- Spread batter in greased 6 x 10-inch
  baking dish and arrange apples in rows over
  top.
- Combine $\frac{1}{2}$ cup sugar, 2 tablespoons flour
  and remaining butter in bowl. Mix until
  crumbly and sprinkle over apples.
- Bake at 350° for 30 minutes or until apples
  are tender and golden brown.

Apple Coffee Cake

1 (18 ounce) box yellow cake mix, divided
1 cup flour
1 (.75 ounce) envelope dry yeast
2 eggs, lightly beaten
1 (20 ounce) can apple pie filling
$\frac{1}{3}$ cup ($\frac{2}{3}$ stick) butter
1 cup powdered sugar

- Stir together $1\frac{1}{2}$ cups cake mix, flour, yeast, $\frac{2}{3}$ cup hot water and eggs.
- Spoon into greased 9 x 13-inch pan and top with pie filling.
- Cut butter into remaining cake mix with fork until crumbly and sprinkle over pie filling.
- Bake at 350° for 25 to 30 minutes. Cool.
- Combine powdered sugar and 1 tablespoon water and drizzle glaze over cake.

Yield: 15 servings.

Mandarin Orange Coffee Cake

1 (18 ounce) box orange cake mix
1 (3.4 ounce) package instant vanilla
  pudding mix
4 eggs
½ cup oil
1 (11 ounce) can mandarin oranges with juice

- Combine cake mix, pudding mix, eggs, oil and juice from mandarin oranges. (Add enough water to juice to make 1 cup liquid.)
- Beat at medium speed for 2 minutes. Add mandarin oranges for last 30 seconds of beating time.
- Pour batter into greased bundt pan.
- Bake at 350° for 40 to 45 minutes or until toothpick inserted in center comes out clean.
- Cool in pan 20 minutes. Invert onto serving plate and dust with powdered sugar.

Yield: 10-12 servings.

Cherry Dome Coffee Cake

1 (12 ounce) can refrigerated dinner rolls
$1/4$ cup butter
$1/4$ cup honey
$1/2$ cup chopped nuts
$1/2$ cup flaked coconut
2 tablespoons grated orange rind
2 tablespoons maraschino cherry halves

- Separate dinner rolls.
- Melt butter, add honey and mix well.
- Combine nuts, coconut, orange rind and cherries and mix well.
- Dip rolls into honey mixture and then nut mixture and place in foil-lined $1^1/2$-quart baking dish.
- Bake at 350° for 40 to 45 minutes or until deep golden brown.
- Invert onto serving plate.

Yield: 12 servings.

Marmalade Kaffee Kuchen

1 (7.5 ounce) can refrigerator biscuits
2 tablespoons (¼ stick) butter, melted
¼ cup orange marmalade
½ cup chopped pecans
1 egg, beaten
½ cup sour cream
1 tablespoon sugar
½ teaspoon vanilla extract

- Roll each biscuit in butter and arrange them in single layer in pan.
- Spoon marmalade onto center of each biscuit and sprinkle with pecans.
- Bake at 450° for 10 minutes.
- Combine egg, sour cream, sugar and vanilla and beat until smooth. Spoon mixture over biscuits.
- Reduce temperature to 350° and bake another 20 minutes. Cut into squares.

Yield: 9 servings.

German Peach Coffee Cake

2 cups flour
3/4 cup sugar, divided
1/4 teaspoon baking powder
1 teaspoon salt
1/2 cup (1 stick) butter
1 (15 ounce) can peach halves, drained
1 teaspoon cinnamon
2 egg yolks, beaten
1 cup sour cream

- Sift flour, 1/4 cup sugar, baking powder and salt. Cut in butter until mixture is crumbly.
- Press mixture firmly into bottom and sides of lightly greased 9-inch springform pan.
- Arrange peaches evenly over crumbs.
- Combine remaining sugar and cinnamon, mix well and sprinkle over peaches.
- Bake at 400° for 15 minutes.
- Blend egg yolks with sour cream and spoon over peaches.
- Bake another 20 minutes or until golden brown.

Yield: 8 servings.

Blueberry Coffee Cake

¾ cup plus 6 tablespoons sugar, divided
¼ cup shortening
1 egg
1 teaspoon vanilla extract
¾ cup milk
1¾ cups flour
3 tablespoons baking powder
½ teaspoon salt
1½ cups blueberries, drained
½ teaspoon cinnamon

- Cream ¾ cup sugar, shortening, egg and vanilla. Add milk and blend well.
- Add flour, baking powder and salt and mix well.
- Spread half of batter in greased 9-inch square baking pan. Cover with blueberries and sprinkle with 2 tablespoons sugar.
- Spread remaining batter over top. Combine cinnamon and 4 tablespoons sugar and sprinkle over batter.
- Bake at 375° for 35 minutes.

Yield: 9 servings.

Apricot Coffee Cake

1 cup shortening
1 cup sugar
1 egg, beaten
1³/₄ cups flour
2 teaspoons baking soda
Dash salt
1 cup milk
1 tablespoon hot water
¹/₂ cup cooked apricots
1 teaspoon vanilla extract

- Cream shortening and sugar and stir in egg.
- Combine flour, baking soda and salt and fold into creamed mixture alternately with milk. Beat until smooth. Stir in water, apricots and vanilla.
- Pour batter into greased 9 x 13-inch pan.
- Bake at 350° for 30 to 40 minutes or until toothpick comes out clean.

Topping:
1 tablespoon butter, melted
³/₄ cup packed brown sugar
³/₄ cup cooked apricots
¹/₂ cup flaked coconut

- Combine ingredients and stir over low heat until they blend well. Spread over warm cake

Apricot-Almond Coffee Cake

1 cup (2 sticks) butter, softened
2 cups sugar
2 eggs
1 cup sour cream
1 teaspoon almond extract
2 cups flour
1 teaspoon baking powder
$\frac{1}{4}$ teaspoon salt
1 cup sliced almonds, divided
1 (10 ounce) jar apricot preserves, divided

- Cream butter and sugar until light and fluffy and beat in eggs.
- Fold in sour cream and almond extract.
- Sift together flour, baking powder and salt and fold into batter.
- Put one-third of batter in greased bundt pan. Sprinkle with half almonds and half preserves.
- Spread on remaining batter, top with remaining preserves and sprinkle with remaining almonds.
- Bake at 350° for 1 hour or until cake tests done.

Cranberry-Nut Coffee Cake

$\frac{1}{4}$ **cup packed brown sugar**
$\frac{1}{2}$ **cup chopped walnuts**
$\frac{1}{4}$ **teaspoon cinnamon**
2 cups biscuit mix
2 tablespoons sugar
1 egg
$\frac{2}{3}$ **cup whole cranberry sauce**

- Mix brown sugar, walnuts and cinnamon and set aside.
- Combine biscuit mix, sugar, egg and $\frac{2}{3}$ cup water (or milk) and beat vigorously for 30 seconds.
- Spread batter in greased 9 x 9-inch pan and sprinkle with brown sugar mixture.
- Spoon cranberry sauce over top.
- Bake at 375° for 20 to 25 minutes.

Glaze:
1 cup powdered sugar
$\frac{1}{2}$ **teaspoon vanilla extract**
1 tablespoon milk

- Combine all glaze ingredients and drizzle over warm coffee cake.

Yield: 9 servings.

Nutty Coffee Cake

1/4 cup packed brown sugar
1/2 teaspoon cinnamon
1/2 teaspoon nutmeg
1/4 cup chopped nuts
1 (18 ounce) box yellow cake mix
1 (3.4 ounce) package instant vanilla
  pudding mix
4 eggs
1 cup sour cream
1 teaspoon vanilla extract

- Mix brown sugar, cinnamon, nutmeg and nuts and set aside.

- Combine cake mix, pudding mix, eggs, sour cream, 1/2 cup water and vanilla. Beat at medium speed for 3 minutes.

- Place half batter in greased bundt pan and top with half of nut mixture. Repeat layers with remaining batter and nut mixture.

- Bake at 350° for 45 to 50 minutes or until toothpick inserted in center of coffee cake comes out clean. Cool in pan for 10 minutes.

Yield: 12 servings.

Streusel-Filled Coffee Cake

3 cups flour
6 teaspoons baking powder
$1/2$ teaspoon salt
$1^1/2$ cups sugar
$1/2$ cup shortening
2 eggs, beaten
1 cup milk
1 teaspoon vanilla extract

Streusel Filling:
3 tablespoons butter, melted
$3/4$ cup packed brown sugar
$3/4$ cup chopped pecans
3 tablespoons flour
3 teaspoons cinnamon

- Sift 3 cups flour, baking powder, salt and sugar. Cut in shortening with pastry blender until mixture is crumbly. (The consistency should be like cornmeal.)

- Combine eggs and milk and blend into flour mixture. Add vanilla. Pour half of batter into well greased cake pan.

- Combine all Streusel Filling ingredients and sprinkle half of mixture over batter in pan. Repeat layers with remaining half batter and half filling mixture.

- Bake at 375° for 25 to 30 minutes.

Coconut-Cream Coffee Cake

1⅓ cups biscuit mix
¾ cup sugar
3 tablespoons shortening
1 teaspoon vanilla extract
1 egg
¾ cup milk, divided
3 tablespoons butter
⅓ cup packed brown sugar
2 tablespoons half-and-half cream
½ cup flaked coconut

- Combine biscuit mix, sugar, shortening, vanilla, egg and ½ cup milk. Beat at medium speed for 1 minute.
- Stir in remaining milk and beat for 30 seconds.
- Pour batter into greased 8 x 8-inch baking pan.
- Bake at 350° for 35 to 40 minutes.
- Combine butter, sugar, half-and-half and coconut. Spread mixture over hot coffee cake.

Yield: 6 servings.

Chocolate Chip Coffee Cake

$^1/_2$ cup (1 stick) butter
$^1/_2$ cup sugar
2 eggs
2 cups flour
$1^1/_2$ teaspoons baking powder
1 teaspoon baking soda
1 (8 ounce) carton sour cream
1 teaspoon vanilla extract
1 (6 ounce) package semi-sweet chocolate
  morsels
1 teaspoon ground cinnamon

- Beat butter at medium speed until creamy. Gradually add sugar and beat mixture well.
- Add eggs one at a time and beat just until yellow disappears.
- Combine flour, baking powder and baking soda.
- Add flour mixture to butter mixture alternately with sour cream. (Be sure to begin and end with flour mixture.)
- Beat at low speed until they blend and stir in vanilla.
- Spread half of batter into greased 9-inch square pan. Sprinkle with chocolate morsels and cinnamon.

(Continued on next page.)

(Continued)

- Spread remaining batter over chocolate layer.
- Bake at 350° for 35 minutes or until cake begins to separate from sides of pan.

Caramel Coffee Cake

1 (25 ounce) package frozen cloverleaf yeast rolls
1 cup packed brown sugar
1 (3.4 ounce) package butterscotch pudding and pie filling mix (not instant)
1 teaspoon cinnamon
$\frac{1}{2}$ cup chopped pecans
$\frac{1}{2}$ cup (1 stick) butter, melted

- Grease bundt pan and fill with cloverleaf rolls. Sprinkle rolls with brown sugar, pudding mix, cinnamon and nuts.
- Pour melted butter over all ingredients.
- Let rise approximately 8 hours or until rolls fill pan.
- Bake at 350° for 35 minutes.
- Invert onto platter to serve.

Yield: 12 servings.

Chocolate Coffee Cake

1¼ cups sugar, divided
4 tablespoons (½ stick) butter, divided
1 egg, beaten
2 cups flour
½ teaspoon baking soda
2 teaspoons baking powder
Pinch of salt
1 cup chocolate milk
½ teaspoon cinnamon

- Cream 1 cup sugar and 2 tablespoons butter. Add egg and mix well.
- Sift flour, baking soda, baking powder and salt and add to creamed mixture alternately with chocolate milk. Beat well after each addition.
- Pour into greased 8-inch square baking pan.
- Melt remaining butter and pour over batter.
- Combine cinnamon and remaining sugar and sprinkle over batter.
- Bake at 350° for 25 to 35 minutes or until toothpick inserted in center of coffee cake comes out clean.

Yield: 8 servings.

Cinnamon-Biscuit Coffee Cake

3 or 4 (7.5 ounce) cans buttermilk biscuits
2 cups sugar, divided
2³/₄ teaspoons cinnamon
¹/₂ cup chopped nuts
³/₄ cup (1¹/₂ sticks) butter

- Cut uncooked biscuits into quarters.
- Combine 1 cup sugar, 1¹/₄ teaspoons cinnamon and nuts and set aside.
- Combine butter, remaining sugar and 1¹/₂ teaspoons cinnamon. Cook over low heat until all ingredients mix well.
- Layer biscuit dough pieces in bundt pan alternating with layers of nut mixture.
- Pour butter mixture over top.
- Bake at 350° for 30 to 40 minutes.
- Invert onto platter to serve.

Sour Cream Coffee Cake

1 cup (2 sticks) butter, softened
1¼ cups sugar
2 eggs
1 cup sour cream
1 teaspoon vanilla extract
2 cups flour
½ teaspoon baking soda
1½ teaspoons baking powder

Topping:
3 tablespoons sugar
1½ teaspoons cinnamon
¾ cup chopped nuts

- Cream butter, sugar and eggs and blend in sour cream and vanilla.
- Sift flour, baking soda and baking powder and add to creamed mixture. Place half of batter into greased bundt pan.
- Combine all topping ingredients and sprinkle half of topping onto batter in pan.
- Add remaining batter and sprinkle with remaining topping.
- Place pan in cold oven. Turn to 350° and bake approximately 55 minutes. Cake is done when toothpick inserted in center comes out clean.

  Yield: 12 servings.

Old-Fashioned Cherry Pie

1 (16 ounce) can pitted cherries with liquid
1 cup sugar
1 tablespoon cornstarch
1 teaspoon fresh lemon juice
¹/₂ teaspoon red food coloring
2 tablespoons (¹/₄ stick) butter
2 (9 inch) unbaked piecrusts

- Drain cherries and reserve liquid.
- In reserved liquid, mix sugar, cornstarch and lemon juice. Stir in cherries and food coloring.
- Pour cherry mixture into unbaked piecrust and dot with butter.
- Cover with second piecrust and slit crust to make air vents.
- Brush top crust with cream and sprinkle with sugar.
- Bake at 350° for about 35 minutes.

Honey Cream-Apple Pie

$1/2$ cup sour cream
$3/4$ cup honey
$1/4$ teaspoon salt
1 teaspoon cinnamon
$1/2$ teaspoon nutmeg
6 large, tart apples, peeled, thinly sliced
2 (9 inch) unbaked piecrusts

- Mix sour cream, honey, salt, cinnamon and nutmeg. Add sliced apples and mix well.
- Pour apple mixture into piecrust and cover with second piecrust. Bake at 400° for 40 to 45 minutes.

Pineapple Pie

1 teaspoon flour
$2/3$ cup sugar
3 eggs, beaten
$1/3$ cup light corn syrup
$1/2$ cup crushed pineapple
$1/3$ cup flaked coconut
$1/3$ cup ($2/3$ stick) butter, softened
1 (9 inch) unbaked piecrust

- Mix flour and sugar, add eggs and mix well.
- Add corn syrup, pineapple, coconut and butter and mix well. Pour mixture into piecrust. Bake at 350° for 40 minutes or until knife comes out clean.

Crispy-Topped Apple Pie

5 to 7 tart apples
2 cups sugar, divided
2 to 3 tablespoons flour
1 teaspoon cinnamon
$1/4$ teaspoon nutmeg
1 (9 inch) unbaked piecrust
$1/2$ cup butter, melted
6 slices bread, crumbled

- Pare and thinly slice apples.
- Mix 1 cup sugar, flour, cinnamon and nutmeg and combine with apples.
- Spoon apple mixture into piecrust.
- In mixing bowl pour butter over crumbled bread.
- Add remaining 1 cup sugar and mix well.
- Dot apple mixture with additional butter and top with crumbled bread mixture.
- Bake at 350° for 30 to 40 minutes.

Mincemeat Pie

1 (28 ounce) jar prepared mincemeat
1$\frac{1}{2}$ cups coarsely chopped walnuts
1 large apple, peeled, diced
$\frac{1}{2}$ cup packed brown sugar
1 tablespoon lemon juice
2 (9 inch) unbaked piecrusts

- Combine mincemeat, walnuts, apple, brown sugar and lemon juice and stir until they blend well.
- Cover and refrigerate overnight allowing flavors to blend.
- Pour mincemeat mixture into piecrust.
- Slice second piecrust into $\frac{1}{2}$-inch strips and arrange over top of pie filling in lattice design.
- Bake at 375° for 35 to 40 minutes.

Double Crust Strawberry Pie

4 (10 ounce) packages frozen strawberry
  halves with juice
½ cup pineapple tidbits, drained
3 tablespoons cornstarch
2 tablespoons sugar
½ teaspoon salt
2 (9 inch) unbaked piecrusts

- Thaw strawberries and reserve ¼ cup liquid.

- Combine strawberries, reserved liquid, pineapple, cornstarch, sugar and salt and blend.

- Pour into piecrust.

- Slice second piecrust into ½-inch strips and arrange in lattice pattern over top of strawberry filling.

- Bake at 400° for 35 to 40 minutes or until golden brown.

Peach Pie with Streusel Topping

1 pint frozen peaches
3/4 cup sugar
2 tablespoons cornstarch
1 (9 inch) unbaked piecrust
2 tablespoons (1/4 stick) butter, divided
1/3 cup packed brown sugar
1/2 cup flour
Sliced almonds

- Thaw, drain peaches and reserve liquid.
- In reserved liquid, mix sugar and cornstarch.
- Add peaches and pour into piecrust. Dot with 1 tablespoon butter.
- In bowl, combine brown sugar, flour and remaining 1 tablespoon butter. Stir until mixture is crumbly.
- Sprinkle streusel topping over pie filling and sprinkle with almonds.
- Bake at 300° for 35 minutes.

Down-Home Pumpkin Pie

3 eggs, slightly beaten
$\frac{1}{2}$ cup sugar
$\frac{1}{2}$ cup packed brown sugar
1 tablespoon flour
$\frac{1}{2}$ teaspoon salt
1 teaspoon cinnamon
$\frac{1}{4}$ teaspoon nutmeg
$\frac{1}{4}$ teaspoon ginger
$\frac{1}{8}$ teaspoon cloves
$1\frac{1}{2}$ cups mashed pumpkin
$1\frac{1}{2}$ cups milk, scalded
1 (9 inch) unbaked piecrust

- Combine eggs, sugars, flour, salt and spices and mix well.
- Add pumpkin and milk, mix well and pour into piecrust.
- Bake at 450° for 10 minutes.
- Reduce to 350° and bake another 40 to 50 minutes or until set. Cool.

Lemon Meringue Pie

1$^1/_3$ cups plus 4 tablespoons sugar, divided
$^1/_2$ cup cornstarch
$^1/_4$ teaspoon plus dash salt, divided
4 eggs, separated
1 tablespoon grated lemon rind
2 tablespoons ($^1/_4$ stick) butter
$^1/_2$ cup lemon juice
1 (9 inch) prepared piecrust
$^1/_2$ teaspoon vanilla extract
$^1/_4$ teaspoon cream of tartar

- Combine 1$^1/_3$ cups sugar, cornstarch and $^1/_4$ teaspoon salt in heavy saucepan.
- Gradually stir in 1$^3/_4$ cups water.
- Bring to boil over medium heat and stir constantly. Boil one minute.
- Remove from heat and stir some of sugar mixture into beaten egg yolks and pour egg yolks into saucepan.
- Add lemon rind, stir constantly for 2 minutes and remove from heat.
- Add butter and stir until it melts.
- Stir in lemon juice and pour into piecrust.
- Beat 4 egg whites with dash salt, vanilla and cream of tartar until frothy.

(Continued on next page.)

(Continued)

- Add 4 tablespoons sugar to egg whites 1 tablespoon at a time and beat mixture until stiff peaks form.
- Spread meringue over pie filling and form into peaks.
- Bake at 375° for 12 minutes.

Lemon-Chess Pie

1²/₃ cups sugar
1 tablespoon flour
1 tablespoon cornmeal
4 eggs
¹/₄ cup (¹/₂ stick) butter, melted
¹/₄ cup milk
¹/₄ cup lemon juice
1 teaspoon grated lemon rind
1 (9 inch) unbaked piecrust

- Combine sugar, flour and cornmeal in bowl and mix lightly with fork.
- Add eggs, butter, milk, lemon juice and lemon rind. Beat until smooth and pour into piecrust.
- Bake at 375° for 35 minutes or until golden brown.

Chocolate Meringue Pie

2 tablespoons flour
2 tablespoons cornstarch
$5/8$ teaspoons salt, divided
$1/2$ cup sugar plus 2 tablespoons sugar, divided
3 tablespoons cocoa
2 cups milk
2 eggs, separated
1 teaspoon vanilla extract
1 (9 inch) prepared piecrust

- In medium saucepan, combine flour, cornstarch, $1/2$ teaspoon salt and $1/2$ cup sugar and add cocoa and milk.
- Cook over medium heat until thick and stir constantly with wire whisk. Add slightly beaten egg yolks and cook 1 minute longer.
- Add vanilla and pour mixture into piecrust.
- Combine $1/8$ teaspoon salt with room temperature egg whites and beat until light but not stiff. Add remaining 2 tablespoons sugar 1 tablespoon at a time and beat well after each addition. Beat until stiff peaks form.
- Spread meringue over chocolate mixture.
- Bake at 325° for 10 to 15 minutes or until meringue is light brown.

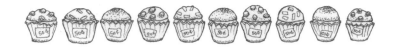

Brownie-Mint Pie

1 (4.6 ounce) package chocolate mints
1 (16 ounce) package brownie mix
1 (9 inch) deep-dish frozen unbaked
  piecrust

- Chop chocolate mints and set aside.
- Prepare brownie batter according to package directions and stir in chopped mints. Pour batter into piecrust.
- Bake at 350° for 45 minutes or until knife inserted in center comes out clean.

Butterscotch Pie

1 cup packed brown sugar
$\frac{1}{3}$ cup flour
3 eggs
2 cups milk
1 tablespoon butter
1 teaspoon vanilla extract
1 (9 inch) unbaked piecrust

- Combine brown sugar, flour, eggs, milk, butter and vanilla and mix well.
- Pour mixture into piecrust.
- Bake at 350° for 40 minutes or until knife inserted in center comes out clean.

Chocolate Crunch Torte

1 cup (2 sticks) butter, softened, divided
1³/₄ cups sugar, divided
3 eggs, separated
2¹/₄ cups flour
3¹/₂ cups ground or finely chopped almonds, toasted
4 (1 ounce) squares semi-sweet baking chocolate, melted
2 teaspoons vanilla extract

- Cream butter and ¹/₄ cup sugar at medium speed and add egg yolks.
- Add flour and blend at low speed until dough forms.
- Press dough into bottom and 1 inch up sides of 10 x 3-inch springform pan.
- Beat egg whites until stiff but not dry.
- Combine almonds, chocolate, remaining 1¹/₂ cups sugar and vanilla.
- Fold egg whites into chocolate mixture and spoon filling over crust.
- Bake at 350° for 40 to 45 minutes or until crust is light golden brown.

Peanut-Coconut Pie

1 cup dark corn syrup
3 eggs
$\frac{1}{2}$ cup sugar
$\frac{1}{2}$ teaspoon vanilla extract
$\frac{1}{4}$ teaspoon salt
$\frac{1}{2}$ cup peanut butter
2 tablespoons ($\frac{1}{4}$ stick) butter, melted
$\frac{1}{2}$ cup flaked coconut
1 cup chopped roasted peanuts
1 (9 inch) unbaked piecrust

- Combine syrup, eggs, sugar, vanilla, salt, peanut butter and butter and beat 1 minute.
- Spread coconut and peanuts in pie shell and pour syrup mixture over top.
- Bake at 400° for 10 minutes.
- Reduce heat to 350° and bake another 20 minutes.

Buttermilk Pie

$^1/_2$ cup (1 stick) butter, softened
2 cups sugar
3 tablespoons flour
$^1/_4$ teaspoon salt
3 eggs
1 cup buttermilk
1 teaspoon vanilla extract
1 (9 inch) unbaked piecrust

- Cream butter, sugar, flour and salt. Add eggs and blend well.
- Stir in buttermilk and vanilla and pour into piecrust.
- Bake at 400° for 10 minutes.
- Reduce temperature to 325°. Bake another 45 minutes or until knife inserted in center comes out clean.

Quick Cherry Pie

½ cup (1 stick) butter
1 cup flour
2 tablespoons plus ½ cup sugar, divided
1 (20 ounce) can cherry pie filling
1 egg

- Melt butter and stir in flour and 2 tablespoons sugar.
- Press mixture into greased 9-inch pie pan to form crust.
- Pour pie filling over crust.
- Combine egg and ½ cup sugar and pour over filling.
- Bake at 350° for 50 to 60 minutes or until top is light brown.

Oatmeal Pie

6 eggs
$\frac{1}{2}$ cup milk
$\frac{1}{4}$ cup ($\frac{1}{2}$ stick) butter, melted
2 cups light corn syrup
1 cup sugar
2 cups oatmeal
$1\frac{1}{2}$ cups flaked coconut
2 (9 inch) unbaked piecrusts

- Combine all ingredients and divide between 2 piecrusts.
- Bake at 350° for 40 to 45 minutes.

Pecan Pie

$\frac{1}{4}$ cup ($\frac{1}{2}$ stick) butter
$\frac{1}{2}$ cup sugar
1 cup light corn syrup
3 eggs
1 cup whole pecans
1 (9 inch) unbaked piecrust

- Cream butter and sugar, stir in syrup and beat well. Add eggs one at a time and beat well after each addition.
- Add pecans and pour mixture into piecrust.
- Bake at 350° for 1 hour 10 minutes or until knife inserted in center comes out clean.

Peanut Brittle

1 cup sugar
$\frac{1}{2}$ cup light corn syrup
$\frac{1}{4}$ teaspoon salt
1 cup shelled peanuts
1 tablespoon butter
1 teaspoon vanilla extract
1 teaspoon baking soda

- Combine sugar, corn syrup, salt and peanuts in glass baking dish and mix well.
- Microwave on MEDIUM-HIGH for 8 minutes or until light brown and turn dish once.
- Add butter and vanilla and mix well.
- Microwave for another $2\frac{1}{2}$ minutes or until mixture reaches hard-crack stage (300° on candy thermometer).
- Stir in baking soda and pour onto greased baking sheet.
- Cool and break into pieces.

Yield: 1 pound.

Peanut Patties

3 cups sugar
1 cup half-and-half cream
$2/3$ cup light corn syrup
2 teaspoons ($1/4$ stick) butter
Pinch salt
2 cups raw peanuts
$1/4$ teaspoon red food coloring
1 teaspoon vanilla extract

- Combine sugar, half-and-half, corn syrup, butter, salt and peanuts in saucepan and bring to boil.
- Lower heat, simmer about 45 minutes or until mixture forms soft ball in cold water and stir occasionally.
- Remove from heat and add food coloring and vanilla. Keep stirring until mixture loses its gloss.
- Drop by teaspoonfuls onto wax paper or into greased muffin pan.

Date Loaf

2 cups sugar
¾ cup milk
1 (16 ounce) package dates, chopped
1 tablespoon butter
1 cup chopped pecans

- Cook sugar and milk to soft-ball stage (234° on candy thermometer).
- Add dates and butter and stir until butter melts.
- Add pecans, remove from heat and stir until mixture becomes thick enough to hold its shape.
- Form mixture into loaf, place on clean, wet cloth and roll. When cold, slice.

Yield: 1 (1.5 x 12") roll.

Fast Turtles

72 pecan halves
24 caramel candies
1 teaspoon shortening
1 (6 ounce) package semi-sweet chocolate chips

- Cover baking sheet with aluminum foil (shiny side up) and grease foil.
- For each candy, place 3 pecan halves in "Y" shape on foil. Place one caramel candy in center of each pecan "Y".
- Bake at 300° just until candy melts, about 9 to 10 minutes.
- Heat shortening and chocolate chips over low heat just until chocolate melts and stir constantly.
- Spread chocolate mixture over candies and leave ends of pecans uncovered.
- Refrigerate until chocolate is firm, about 30 minutes.

Yield: 24 candies.

Cinnamon Pralines

1½ cups sugar
¾ cup packed brown sugar
½ cup (1 stick) butter
½ cup milk
1 teaspoon ground cinnamon
1½ cups pecan halves

- Cook all ingredients in heavy 3-quart saucepan over low heat and stir constantly until sugars dissolve and butter melts.
- Bring mixture to boil over medium heat and cook, stirring constantly, for 3 minutes or until candy thermometer reaches 230°.
- Remove from heat and stir mixture with wooden spoon for 6 minutes or until it begins to thicken.
- Drop by tablespoonfuls onto wax paper coated with non-stick spray. (Work fast.)
- Let stand until firm.

Yield: 30 pralines.

English Toffee

1⅓ cups sugar
1 cup (2 sticks) butter, melted
1 tablespoon light corn syrup
2 tablespoons water
1½ teaspoons vanilla extract
½ cup chocolate chips
½ cup chopped walnuts

- Combine sugar, butter, corn syrup and water in 2-quart glass baking dish.
- Microwave on HIGH for 10-12 minutes or until caramel-colored and stir twice.
- Quickly stir in vanilla and pour mixture into buttered 9 x 12-inch dish.
- Sprinkle chocolate chips over top, let stand until chips are soft and spread chocolate evenly.
- Sprinkle with walnuts and set in cool place until firm. Break into pieces.

Yield: 1½ pounds.

Tip: You must use real butter for this recipe—
no substitutions.

Chocolate-Peanut Butter Balls

1 (8 ounce) jar crunchy peanut butter
$\frac{1}{2}$ cup (1 stick) butter, softened
3 cups powdered sugar
1 (9 ounce) bar milk chocolate
$\frac{1}{4}$ bar paraffin

- Mix peanut butter, butter and powdered sugar by hand. Form into small balls.
- Melt chocolate bar with paraffin over low heat. Dip balls into chocolate mixture and cool on wax paper.
- Refrigerate until firm. Yield: 48 balls.

Orange-Coconut Balls

These are very simple, no-bake cookies.

1 (12 ounce) box vanilla wafers, crushed
$\frac{1}{2}$ cup (1 stick) butter, softened
1 (12 ounce) can frozen orange juice concentrate
1 (16 ounce) box powdered sugar
1 cup chopped pecans
1 cup flaked coconut

- Mix all ingredients and form into balls.
- Roll in more powdered sugar and let stand.

Chocolate Crunchies

1 (6 ounce) package butterscotch chips
1 (6 ounce) package chocolate chips
1 (8 ounce) can dry-roasted peanuts
1 (5 ounce) can chow mein noodles

- Melt butterscotch and chocolate chips in skillet over low heat.
- Add peanuts and noodles and stir until they completely blend.
- Drop by tablespoonfuls onto wax paper.
- Refrigerate about 1 hour or until firm. Yield: 36 candies.

Peanut Butter Fudge

2 cups sugar
²/₃ cup milk
1 pint marshmallow cream
1 cup crunchy peanut butter
1 teaspoon vanilla extract

- Cook sugar and milk until mixture forms soft ball in cold water.
- Add marshmallow cream, peanut butter and vanilla and stir until they blend well.
- Pour into greased 9-inch square pan.

Rocky Road Fudge

1 (12 ounce) package semi-sweet chocolate
  morsels
1 (14 ounce) can sweetened condensed milk
2 tablespoons ($^{1}/_{4}$ stick) butter
2 cups dry-roasted peanuts
1 (10.5 ounce) package miniature
  marshmallows

- Place chocolate morsels, sweetened condensed milk, and butter in top of double boiler and bring to boil.
- Reduce heat to low, cook until chocolate and butter melt and stir constantly.
- Remove from heat and stir in peanuts and marshmallows.
- Spread mixture into wax paper-lined 9 x 13-inch baking pan.
- Chill at least 2 hours before cutting into $1^{1}/_{2}$-inch squares.

Yield: 48 pieces.

Vanilla Fudge

2 cups sugar
$\frac{1}{3}$ cup light corn syrup
2 tablespoons ($\frac{1}{4}$ stick) butter
$\frac{1}{2}$ cup sour cream
Pinch of salt
2 teaspoons vanilla extract
1 cup chopped pecans

- Combine sugar, corn syrup, butter, sour cream and salt in saucepan. Cook over low heat until sugar dissolves completely and stir constantly.
- Cook, covered, over medium heat for 3 minutes or until steam washes sugar crystals from side of pan.
- Cook, uncovered, over medium heat until mixture reaches soft-ball stage (230° on candy thermometer). Do not stir.
- Remove from heat and let stand 15 minutes.
- Add vanilla and pecans and beat until mixture thickens and loses its gloss.
- Pour into buttered 9-inch dish, cool and cut into squares.

Yield: 24 pieces.

Chocolate-Marshmallow Fudge

3 cups sugar
$^3/_4$ cup (1$^1/_2$ sticks) butter
$^2/_3$ cup evaporated milk
1 (12 ounce) package chocolate chips
1 (17 ounce) jar marshmallow cream
1 cup chopped pecans, optional
1 teaspoon vanilla extract

- Combine sugar, butter and milk in medium saucepan.
- Bring to boil and stir constantly. Boil for 5 minutes.
- Remove saucepan from heat and stir in chocolate chips until they melt.
- Add marshmallow cream, pecans and vanilla and beat until ingredients blend.
- Pour into greased 9 x 13-inch pan. Cool and cut into squares.

Yield: 18 to 20 pieces.

Chocolate-Covered Cherries

$^1/_3$ cup ($^2/_3$ stick) butter, softened
$2^1/_4$ cups powdered sugar
$1-1^1/_2$ teaspoons milk
2 teaspoons cherry liqueur
2 (10 ounce) jars maraschino cherries with
   stems, drained
1 (8 ounce) package semi-sweet chocolate
   squares
1 tablespoon shortening

- Beat butter at medium speed until creamy, gradually add powdered sugar and beat well.

- Mix in milk and liqueur until blended.

- Coat cherries completely with butter mixture and place on wax paper.

- Microwave chocolate and shortening in 2-cup glass measuring cup on HIGH for 1 minute 30 seconds or until it melts and stir twice.

- Dip coated cherries by stems into chocolate mixture and allow excess chocolate to drip off of cherries.

- Place cherries on wax paper and set aside until firm.

   Yield: 36 candies.

Cherry-Honey Divinity

2 cups sugar
1/3 cup honey
2 egg whites, well beaten
1/4 cup candied cherries, chopped

- Place sugar, honey and 1/3 cup water in 2-quart saucepan.
- Bring to boil over medium heat and cook until syrup spins a thread.
- Slowly pour syrup over egg whites while beating constantly with electric mixer.
- Continue to beat until candy begins to lose its glaze.
- Fold in cherries.
- Drop by teaspoonfuls onto wax paper.

Yield: 30 candies.

Old-Fashioned Taffy

1 cup packed brown sugar
$\frac{1}{4}$ cup light corn syrup
$\frac{1}{3}$ cup water
1 tablespoon butter
$\frac{1}{8}$ teaspoon salt
$\frac{3}{4}$ teaspoon vanilla extract

- Boil brown sugar, corn syrup, water, butter and salt until mixture forms a hard ball in cold water or reaches the soft-crack stage (275° on candy thermometer).

- Remove from heat, add vanilla and pour into well greased pan.

- When cool enough to handle, pull and twist until golden.

- Cut into pieces with scissors and wrap individually in wax paper or plastic wrap.

Peppermint Patties

1 (16 ounce) box powdered sugar
3 tablespoons butter
2 to 3 teaspoons peppermint extract
$\frac{1}{2}$ teaspoon vanilla extract
$\frac{1}{4}$ cup evaporated milk
2 cups semi-sweet chocolate chips
2 tablespoons shortening

- Combine powdered sugar, butter and extracts. Add milk and mix well.
- Roll into 1-inch balls, place on wax paper-lined baking sheet and chill 20 minutes.
- Melt chocolate chips and shortening in microwave and stir to combine.
- Dip patties in chocolate mixture, place on wax paper and cool.

Yield: 60 candies.

Almond-Butter Circle

½ cup (1 stick) butter
1 teaspoon corn syrup
½ cup sugar
1 cup slivered almonds, blanched

- Line 8 or 9-inch round cake pan with foil and butter foil liberally.
- Combine all ingredients in 10-inch skillet.
- Bring to boil over medium heat and boil 5-6 minutes. (The mixture will be amber-colored.)
- Pour mixture into pan and cool for 15 minutes.
- Remove from foil and break into pieces.

Ritz Cracker Cookies

1 (14 ounce) can sweetened condensed milk
1 cup chopped dates
½ cup ground pecans
About 40 Ritz crackers

- Combine sweetened condensed milk, dates and pecans and stir constantly to form paste.
- Spread about 1 teaspoon paste on each cracker.

Frosting:
1 (3 ounce) package cream cheese
¾ stick butter
3 cups powdered sugar
1 teaspoon vanilla extract

- Stir all frosting ingredients until they blend well and top each cracker with frosting.

Yield: about 40 cookies.

Do-Little Butterscotch Macaroons

½ cup flour
1 (3.9 ounce) package instant butterscotch
  pudding mix
2 cups flaked coconut
1 cup sweetened condensed milk
½ teaspoon almond extract

- Combine all ingredients and mix well.
- Drop by teaspoonfuls onto greased baking sheet 2 inches apart.
- Bake at 325° for 10 to 12 minutes.
  Yield: 30 cookies.

Sand Tarts

1 cup (2 sticks) butter
¾ cup powdered sugar
2 teaspoons vanilla extract
1 cup very finely chopped pecans
2 cups flour

- Cream butter, powdered sugar, and vanilla.
- Gradually add pecans, mix well and stir in flour. Roll the dough into balls or crescents and arrange on baking sheet.
- Bake at 325° for 15 minutes. Roll in additional powdered sugar.
  Yield: 48 cookies.

Cherry-Coconut Cookies

1 cup packed brown sugar
1 cup sugar
1 cup shortening
2 eggs
2$\frac{1}{2}$ cups flour
1 teaspoon baking soda
1 teaspoon salt
1 teaspoon vanilla extract
1 cup chopped maraschino cherries, well
  drained
$\frac{1}{2}$ cup flaked coconut

- Cream both sugars, shortening and eggs.
- Combine flour, baking soda and salt.
- Add flour mixture to sugar mixture a little at a time and mix well after each addition.
- Add cherries and coconut. Mix well and drop by tablespoonfuls onto greased baking sheet.
- Bake at 350° for 15 to 18 minutes.

Yield: 48 cookies.

Pick-A-Cereal Cookies
Use your favorite cereals to make different cookies.

$^2/_3$ cup butter-flavored shortening
$^1/_2$ cup sugar
$^1/_2$ cup packed brown sugar
1 egg
1 teaspoon vanilla extract
$1^1/_4$ cups flour
$^1/_2$ teaspoon baking soda
$^1/_2$ teaspoon salt
1 cup cereal

- Cream shortening and both sugars until light and fluffy and blend in egg and vanilla.
- Combine flour, baking soda and salt and add to creamed mixture.
- Stir in cereal and drop dough by teaspoonfuls onto ungreased baking sheet.
- Bake at 375° for 8 to 10 minutes.

Yield: 36 cookies.

Almond-Butter Cookies

1 cup (2 sticks) butter, softened
1/2 cup sugar
1/4 teaspoon salt
2 cups flour
1 teaspoon almond extract

- Cream butter and sugar and add salt, flour and almond extract. Mix well.
- Chill until dough is easy to handle.
- Form 1-inch balls, roll balls in additional sugar and flatten.
- Bake at 350° for 12 to 15 minutes.

Yield: 36 cookies.

Tip: If you prefer, dough can be rolled out to 1/4-inch thickness for use with a cookie cutter.

White Chocolate Chunk Macadamia Cookies

$^2/_3$ cup (1$^1/_3$ sticks) butter, softened
$^1/_2$ cup sugar
$^1/_2$ cup packed brown sugar
1 egg
1 teaspoon vanilla extract
1$^1/_2$ cups flour
1 (3.5 ounce) jar macadamia nuts, coarsely chopped
2 (3 ounce) bars white chocolate, chopped in $^1/_2$-inch pieces

- Cream butter, both sugars, egg and vanilla until fluffy.
- Add flour and beat until they blend.
- Stir in nuts and chocolate.
- Drop dough by heaping tablespoons onto greased baking sheet 2$^1/_2$ inches apart.
- Bake at 325° for 17 minutes.

Yield: 24 to 36 cookies.

Forget 'em Cookies

2 egg whites, room temperature
Dash of salt
¾ cup sugar
1 teaspoon vanilla extract
1 (6 ounce) package semi-sweet chocolate
  morsels
1 cup chopped pecans

- Preheat oven to 350°.
- Beat egg whites on high speed until foamy and add salt.
- Gradually add sugar 1 tablespoon at a time and beat until stiff peaks form.
- Fold vanilla, chocolate morsels and pecans into egg white mixture.
- Drop dough by teaspoonfuls onto greased baking sheet.
- Place baking sheet in oven and immediately TURN OFF HEAT. Do not open oven door for at least 8 hours.

Yield: 36 cookies.

Chewy Chocolate Cookies

4 tablespoons ($\frac{1}{2}$ stick) butter
1 (6 ounce) package semi-sweet chocolate
   morsels
1 (14 ounce) can sweetened condensed milk
1 cup flour
1 teaspoon vanilla extract
$\frac{1}{2}$ cup chopped pecans

- Melt butter and chocolate chips over low heat.
- Add condensed milk and stir until ingredients blend well.
- Add flour, vanilla and pecans and mix well.
- Drop dough by teaspoonfuls onto greased baking sheet.
- Bake at 350° for 8 to 10 minutes.

   Yield: 48 cookies.

Jumbo Chocolate Chip Cookies

$^1/_2$ cup (1 stick) butter, softened
$^1/_2$ cup shortening
1 cup packed brown sugar
$^1/_2$ cup sugar
2 eggs
2 teaspoon vanilla extract
$2^1/_2$ cups flour
1 teaspoon baking soda
$^1/_2$ teaspoon salt
1 (12 ounce) package semi-sweet chocolate
  morsels

- Cream butter and shortening until light.
- Gradually add both sugars and beat well after each addition.
- Blend in eggs and vanilla.
- Combine flour, baking soda and salt and add flour mixture to butter mixture 1 cup at a time. Mix well.
- Stir in chocolate morsels.
- Drop onto ungreased baking sheet. (Use scant $^1/_4$ cup dough for each cookie.)
- Bake at 375° for 10 to 12 minutes.

Yield: 30 cookies.

Peanutty Chocolate Surprises

1 cup smooth peanut butter
$1/2$ cup (1 stick) butter, softened
1 cup packed brown sugar
2 eggs
1 cup flour
1 teaspoon baking powder
1 teaspoon cinnamon
1 (16 ounce) package milk chocolate kisses
Powdered sugar

- Cream peanut butter, butter and brown sugar and beat in eggs.
- Combine flour, baking powder and cinnamon and add gradually to creamed mixture until they blend well.
- Chill dough at least 30 minutes for easy handling.
- Form 1 teaspoon dough around each chocolate kiss and place on ungreased baking sheet.
- Bake at 350° for 10 to 12 minutes. Roll in powdered sugar.

Yield: 96 cookies.

Peanut Butter Criss-Crosses

1 cup shortening
1 cup sugar
1 cup packed brown sugar
1 teaspoon vanilla extract
2 eggs, beaten
1 cup smooth peanut butter
3 cups flour
2 teaspoons baking soda
Dash salt

- Cream shortening, both sugars and vanilla and add eggs.
- Stir peanut butter into shortening mixture.
- Sift together flour, baking soda and salt and stir into shortening mixture.
- Form dough into tiny balls, place on greased baking sheet and press with back of fork to make criss-cross pattern.
- Bake at 375° for 10 minutes.

Yield: 96 cookies.

Pound Cake Cookies

1 cup sugar
1 cup (2 sticks) butter, softened
2 cups flour
1 egg yolk
1 teaspoon rum
$^{1}/_{2}$ teaspoon salt
$^{1}/_{2}$ teaspoon vanilla extract
Pecan halves

- Cream sugar and butter, add flour and egg yolk and beat well.
- Stir in rum, salt and vanilla.
- Chill, covered, until firm.
- Shape dough into $^{1}/_{2}$-inch balls and place on non-stick baking sheet.
- Press 1 pecan half into each cookie.
- Bake at 350° for 10 minutes.

Yield: 24 to 36 cookies.

Texas Tea Cakes

2 cups sugar
1 cup (2 sticks) butter, softened
2 eggs
2 teaspoons vanilla extract
Milk
4 cups flour
2 tablespoons baking powder

- Cream sugar and butter until light and fluffy.
- Beat eggs, add vanilla and enough milk to make 1 cup liquid and add to creamed mixture.
- Add flour and baking powder and mix well.
- Refrigerate dough about 30 minutes for easier handling.
- Roll dough to $\frac{1}{2}$-inch thickness on floured board, cut into desired shapes and place cookies on greased baking sheet.
- Bake at 350° for 10 minutes.

Yield: 30 cookies.

Chocolate-Oatmeal Cookies

1/2 cup (1 stick) butter
4 tablespoons cocoa
2 cups sugar
1/2 cup milk
1/2 cup peanut butter
3 cups oatmeal, uncooked
1 teaspoon vanilla extract

- Combine butter, cocoa, sugar and milk in 2-quart saucepan. Bring to boil and boil for 2 minutes. Remove from heat, add peanut butter, oatmeal and vanilla and mix well.
- Drop by teaspoonfuls onto wax paper.
  Yield: 24 cookies.

Lemon Crispies

1 (18 ounce) box lemon cake mix
1/2 cup (1 stick) butter, melted
1 egg, beaten
1 cup crispy rice cereal

- Combine cake mix, butter, and egg and gently stir in cereal.
- Roll dough into 1 1/2-inch balls and place balls 2 inches apart on ungreased baking sheet.
- Bake at 350° for 1 minute.
  Yield: 25 to 30 cookies.

Old-Fashioned Sugar Cookies

1 cup (2 sticks) butter, softened
1 cup sugar
1 egg
1 teaspoon vanilla extract
2$\frac{1}{2}$ cups flour
1 teaspoon baking soda
$\frac{1}{4}$ teaspoon salt

- Cream butter and sugar and add egg and vanilla.
- Add flour, baking soda and salt and mix well.
- Form dough into balls, press down with glass dipped in sugar and place on baking sheet.
- Bake at 350° for 7 to 10 minutes.

Yield: 36 cookies.

Old-Fashioned Gingersnaps

1¼ cups sugar, divided
2 cups flour
½ teaspoon salt
1 teaspoon cinnamon
1 teaspoon baking soda
1 teaspoon ground ginger
½ teaspoon ground cloves
¾ cup shortening
¼ cup molasses
1 egg, lightly beaten

- Combine 1 cup sugar, flour, salt, cinnamon, baking soda, ginger and cloves. Cut in shortening until mixture resembles coarse crumbs.
- Stir in molasses and egg.
- Shape dough into 1-inch balls and roll in remaining ¼ cup sugar. Place balls 2 inches apart on ungreased baking sheet.
- Bake at 350° for 10 minutes.

Yield: 48 to 50 cookies.

Potato Chip Cookies

1 pound butter
1 cup sugar
³/₄ cup crushed potato chips
1 teaspoon vanilla extract
3 cups flour
1 cup chopped pecans

- Cream butter and sugar and beat in potato chips and vanilla. Slowly add flour and pecans.
- Drop by teaspoonfuls onto greased baking sheet.
- Bake at 350° for 15 to 18 minutes.

Yield: 48 cookies.

Chocolate-Coconut Brownies

2 cups sugar
1½ cups flour
½ cup cocoa
⅔ cup oil
4 eggs
1 teaspoon salt
2 teaspoons vanilla extract
1 (14 ounce) can sweetened condensed milk
1 (12 ounce) package flaked coconut
1 (16 ounce) carton prepared chocolate
  frosting

- Beat sugar, flour, cocoa, oil, eggs, salt and vanilla at medium speed until smooth.
- Spread batter into greased 9 x 13-inch baking pan.
- Bake at 350° for 25 minutes.
- Combine sweetened condensed milk and coconut, spread mixture over warm brownies and bake another 10 minutes.
- Cool completely. Spread frosting over brownies.

Yield: 36 brownies.

Melt-Away Brownies

1 (18 ounce) package refrigerated
  chocolate chip cookie dough
4$\frac{1}{2}$ (2 ounce) Milky Way candy bars, sliced
$\frac{1}{2}$ cup crushed corn flakes
$\frac{1}{2}$ cup chopped nuts

- Cut cookie dough into $\frac{1}{4}$-inch slices. Place slices in bottom of ungreased

  9 x 13-inch baking dish and press dough together to form flat crust.
- Bake at 375° for 12 to 15 minutes or until golden brown.
- Remove from oven and arrange candy bar slices over crust. Return to oven for 2 to 3 minutes or until candy softens.
- With spatula, quickly spread candy evenly over entire surface. Sprinkle with corn flakes and nuts and press in slightly. Cool and cut into bars.

Yield: 36 brownies.

Brickle Brownies

1 cup (2 sticks) butter
4 (1 ounce) squares unsweetened baking
  chocolate
4 eggs
2 cups sugar
2 cups flour
$\frac{1}{2}$ teaspoon salt
1 teaspoon vanilla extract
$1\frac{1}{2}$ cups chopped pecans
1 cup brickle bits

- Melt butter and baking chocolate and set aside.
- Beat eggs, gradually add sugar and mix well.
- Add flour, salt and vanilla to egg mixture and beat well.
- Stir in chocolate mixture, pecans and brickle bits.
- Pour batter into greased 9 x 13-inch baking pan.
- Bake at 325° for 40 to 45 minutes.

Yield: 30 brownies

Chocolate Chip-Meringue Brownies

1½ cups flour
1½ cups packed brown sugar, divided
½ cup (1 stick) butter, melted
1 (6 ounce) package semi-sweet chocolate morsels
1½ cups chopped pecans
3 egg whites, room temperature

- Combine flour and ½ cup packed brown sugar. Stir in butter and blend well.

- Press mixture into ungreased 9 x 13-inch baking pan and sprinkle with chocolate morsels and pecans.

- Beat egg whites at high speed until foamy. Gradually add 1 cup packed brown sugar and beat until stiff peaks form.

- Spread meringue over chocolate and pecans.

- Bake at 375° for 18 to 20 minutes.

Yield: 36 brownies.

Layered Mint Brownies

Layer #1:
1 cup sugar
$^{1}/_{2}$ cup (1 stick) butter
4 eggs
1 (16 ounce) can chocolate syrup
1 cup flour
$^{1}/_{2}$ teaspoon baking powder
$^{1}/_{4}$ teaspoon salt

- Mix all ingredients and pour batter into greased 9 x 13-inch baking pan.
- Bake at 350° for 25 minutes.

Layer #2:
$^{1}/_{2}$ cup (1 stick) butter, softened
1 teaspoon peppermint extract
2 cups powdered sugar
Green food coloring, optional

- Mix all ingredients and spread on cool brownies.

Layer #3:
$^{1}/_{2}$ cup (1 stick) butter
1 (6 ounce) package semi-sweet chocolate chips

- Melt together, stir both ingredients and pour over second layer.
Yield: 36 brownies.

Chocolate-Mint Brownies

2 (1 ounce) squares unsweetened baking
  chocolate
$\frac{1}{2}$ cup (1 stick) butter
1 cup sugar
$\frac{1}{4}$ teaspoon salt
$\frac{1}{4}$ teaspoon peppermint extract
1 teaspoon vanilla extract
2 eggs, beaten
$\frac{1}{2}$ cup flour

- Melt baking chocolate and butter over low heat. Let cool for 10 minutes.
- Stir in sugar, salt, peppermint and vanilla.
- Beat in eggs one at a time and mix in flour.
- Pour batter into greased 9-inch square pan.
- Bake at 350° for 20 to 25 minutes or until toothpick comes out clean. Cool completely.

Frosting:
2 tablespoons ($\frac{1}{4}$ stick) butter, softened
2 tablespoons whipping cream
1$\frac{1}{2}$ cups powdered sugar
$\frac{1}{2}$ teaspoon peppermint extract

- Combine frosting ingredients in medium bowl and stir until smooth. Spread on cool brownies. Yield: 8 brownies.

Kahlua Brownies

4 (1 ounce) squares unsweetened baking
   chocolate
1 cup (2 sticks) butter
2 cups sugar
4 eggs
2 teaspoons kahlua
1 cup flour
1 cup semi-sweet chocolate morsels
1 cup chopped nuts

- Melt baking chocolate and butter over low heat and stir constantly. Remove from heat and cool for 8 to 10 minutes.
- Stir in sugar and beat in eggs one at a time. Add kahlua and flour and mix well.
- Stir in chocolate chips and nuts and pour into greased 9 x 13-inch baking pan.
- Bake at 325° for 35 minutes or until edges are firm. Cool for 30 to 60 minutes.

Yield: 48 brownies.

Blonde Chocolate Chip Brownies

²/₃ cup oil
2 cups packed brown sugar
2 teaspoons vanilla extract
2 eggs
2 cups flour
1 teaspoon baking powder
¹/₄ teaspoon baking soda
1 teaspoon salt
1 (12 ounce) package chocolate chips

- Combine oil, brown sugar, 2 tablespoons hot water, vanilla and eggs and set aside.
- Combine flour, baking powder, baking soda and salt.
- Add small amounts of flour mixture to oil mixture and combine well after each addition.
- Spread in greased 9 x 13-inch baking pan and sprinkle chocolate chips over top.
- Bake at 350° for 25 to 30 minutes.

Yield: 48 brownies.

White Chocolate Brownies

1 cup (2 sticks) butter
8 (2 ounce) white chocolate bars, chopped
4 eggs
$1/4$ teaspoon salt
1 cup sugar
1 tablespoon vanilla extract
2 cups flour
1 (8 ounce) package semi-sweet chocolate
  squares, chopped
1 cup chopped macadamia nuts

- Melt butter over low heat and add half of white chocolate. Do not stir.

- Beat eggs and salt at high speed until mixture thickens slightly. Add sugar and beat 2 to 3 minutes or until fluffy.

- Add butter mixture, vanilla and flour. Beat until smooth.

- Fold in remaining white chocolate, semi-sweet chocolate pieces and nuts. Spoon batter into greased 9 x 13-inch baking pan.

- Bake at 350° for 30 to 35 minutes or until light brown. Cool.

  Yield: 30 brownies.

Raspberry Brownies

1 cup (2 sticks) butter
4 (1 ounce) squares unsweetened baking
  chocolate
4 eggs
2 cups sugar
2 cups flour
$\frac{1}{2}$ teaspoon salt
1 teaspoon vanilla extract
1 cup fresh raspberries
$\frac{1}{2}$ cup raspberry jam
Powdered sugar

- Melt butter and baking chocolate and set aside.
- Beat eggs and gradually add sugar. Add flour, salt and vanilla to egg mixture and beat well.
- Stir in chocolate mixture.
- Fold in raspberries and pour into 9 x 13-inch baking pan. Melt raspberry jam, drizzle over batter and swirl with knife.
- Bake at 325° for 40 to 45 minutes and sprinkle with powdered sugar.

Yield: 30 brownies.

Chocolate-Cherry Brownies

1 (18 ounce) box chocolate fudge cake mix
1 (20 ounce) can cherry pie filling
1 teaspoon almond extract
2 eggs, beaten
1 cup sugar
5 tablespoons ($^2/_3$ stick) butter
$^1/_3$ cup milk
$^1/_3$ cup cocoa

- Combine cake mix, pie filling, almond extract and eggs. Mix well and pour into greased 9 x 13-inch baking pan.
- Bake at 375° for 20 to 30 minutes or until toothpick inserted in center comes out clean.
- Combine sugar, butter, milk and cocoa. Bring to boil and boil for 1 minute. Pour over baked layer.

Yield: 36 brownies

German Chocolate Brownies

1 (18 ounce) box German chocolate cake
mix
$\frac{1}{2}$ cup (1 stick) butter, melted
2 eggs, slightly beaten
1 cup flaked coconut
1 (16 ounce) box powdered sugar
1 (8 ounce) package cream cheese
1 (6 ounce) package miniature semi-sweet
chocolate chips

- Combine cake mix, butter, eggs and coconut and mix well.
- Spread in greased 9 x 13-inch baking pan.
- Cream powdered sugar and cream cheese and spread over chocolate batter. Sprinkle chocolate chips over top.
- Bake at 350° for 40 minutes.

Yield: 12 brownies.

Caramel-Fudge Brownies

1 (14 ounce) package caramels
²/₃ cup evaporated milk, divided
1 (18 ounce) box devil's food cake mix
³/₄ cup (1¹/₂ sticks) butter, melted
1¹/₂ cups semi-sweet chocolate chips

- Melt caramels with ¹/₃ cup evaporated milk over low heat and keep warm.
- Combine cake mix, butter and remaining ¹/₃ cup evaporated milk. Stir until dough begins to stick together.
- Press two-thirds of mixture into greased 9 x 13-inch baking pan.
- Bake at 350° for 6 minutes.
- Remove from oven and cover brownie layer with chocolate chips. Spoon melted caramels over chocolate.
- Press remaining dough mixture over caramel layer.
- Bake another 20 to 25 minutes or until toothpick inserted in center comes out clean.

Yield: 16 large or 40 small brownies.

Frosted Caramel Brownies

1 (18 ounce) box yellow cake mix
1 cup chopped nuts
$\frac{1}{2}$ cup shortening
2 eggs
1 cup caramel ice cream topping
2 tablespoons hot water

- Combine all brownie ingredients.
- Beat at medium speed until creamy, about 3 minutes. Spread batter into ungreased jellyroll pan.
- Bake at 325° for 30 to 40 minutes or until top springs back when touched lightly in center. Cool completely.

Frosting:
2 cups powdered sugar
$\frac{1}{3}$ cup ($\frac{2}{3}$ stick) butter
3 tablespoons caramel ice cream topping
2 tablespoons milk

- In small mixing bowl, combine all frosting ingredients. Beat at medium speed until smooth, about 2 minutes. Spread on cooled brownies.

Yield: 36 brownies.

Corn Syrup Brownies

⅔ cup oil
2 cups sugar
⅓ cup light corn syrup
4 eggs, beaten
½ cup cocoa
1½ cups flour
½ teaspoon salt
1 teaspoon baking powder
2 teaspoons vanilla extract

- Beat oil, sugar, corn syrup and eggs.
- Add cocoa, flour, salt, baking powder and vanilla and beat well.
- Pour batter into greased 9 x 13-inch baking pan.
- Bake at 350° for 45 minutes.

Yield: 36 brownies.

Apple Brownies

½ cup (1 stick) butter, softened
1 cup sugar
1 egg
1 cup flour
½ teaspoon baking soda
½ teaspoon baking powder
¼ teaspoon salt
1 teaspoon cinnamon
2 cups thinly sliced or finely chopped, peeled apples

- Combine butter, sugar, egg, flour, baking soda, baking powder, salt and cinnamon. Mix until smooth.
- Stir in apples and spread batter into greased 9-inch square pan.
- Bake at 350° for 35 to 40 minutes or until toothpick inserted in center comes out clean. Cool.

Yield: 18 brownies.

Crispy Brownies

½ cup (1 stick) butter
1 (12 ounce) package chocolate chips,
  divided
1 cup peanut butter
1 (10 ounce) package miniature
  marshmallows
4½ cups crispy rice cereal
1 cup peanuts
1 (6 ounce) package butterscotch chips

- Combine butter, half chocolate chips and peanut butter in saucepan. Cook over low heat until ingredients melt and stir until smooth.
- Add marshmallows and stir until they melt.
- Blend in cereal and peanuts and spread in 9 x 13-inch pan. Chill until firm.
- Melt remaining chocolate chips and butterscotch chips together and blend until smooth. Spread on chilled cereal mixture and cut into 1 x 2-inch bars.

Yield: 60 brownies.

Pumpkin Brownies

4 eggs, beaten
1 cup oil
1 3/4 cups sugar
1/2 teaspoon salt
1 cup pumpkin
2 teaspoons cinnamon
1 teaspoon baking soda
1 teaspoon baking powder
2 cups flour

- Combine all brownie ingredients and pour batter into greased jellyroll pan.
- Bake at 350° for 20 to 25 minutes.

Frosting:
1 (3 ounce) package cream cheese, softened
4 tablespoons (1/2 stick) butter
1 1/2 cups powdered sugar
1 teaspoon milk
1 teaspoon vanilla extract

- Beat all frosting ingredients until fluffy and spread over cool brownies.

Yield: 48 brownies.

Pecan Mini-Muffins

½ cup (1 stick) butter
2 eggs, beaten
1 cup packed dark brown sugar
½ cup flour
1 teaspoon vanilla extract
1½ cups chopped pecans

- Melt butter and add eggs and brown sugar. Mix with spoon.
- Stir in flour, vanilla and pecans and mix well.
- Pour batter into greased miniature muffin pans.
- Bake at 350° for 20 minutes.

Yield: 24 miniature muffins.

Pecan-Orange Muffins

½ cup (1 stick) butter, softened
1 cup plus 1 tablespoon sugar
2 eggs
2 cups flour
1 teaspoon baking soda
1 (8 ounce) container plain yogurt
¾ cup chopped pecans, toasted
1 teaspoon grated orange rind
¼ cup orange juice

- Beat butter until creamy, gradually add 1 cup sugar and beat well.
- Add eggs one at a time and beat after each addition. Combine flour and baking soda.
- Add flour mixture to butter mixture alternately with yogurt. (Begin and end with flour mixture.) Beat well on low speed after each addition.
- Stir in pecans and orange rind.
- Pour batter into greased muffin pan.
- Bake at 375° for 18 to 20 minutes or until light brown. Brush orange juice over hot muffins and sprinkle with remaining 1 tablespoon sugar.

Yield: 12 muffins.

Lemon-Walnut Muffins

$^1/_2$ cup (1 stick) butter
1 cup plus 4 teaspoons sugar
2 large eggs
1 teaspoon baking soda
2 teaspoons grated lemon peel
2 cups flour, divided
1 cup buttermilk, divided
$^1/_2$ cup chopped walnuts
$^1/_4$ cup freshly squeezed lemon juice

- Cream butter and 1 cup sugar, add eggs and beat well.
- Stir in baking soda and lemon peel.
- Fold in 1 cup flour and $^1/_2$ cup buttermilk, stir and fold in remaining flour and buttermilk.
- Add walnuts and stir.
- Pour batter into greased muffin pan. (Place about $^1/_4$ cup batter in each cup.)
- Bake at 375° for 20 to 25 minutes.
- Remove from oven, brush muffin tops with lemon juice and sprinkle with remaining

  4 teaspoons sugar.

Yield: 12-16 muffins.

Cranberry-Almond Muffins

1½ cups flour
½ cup sugar
1 teaspoon baking powder
¼ teaspoon baking soda
¼ teaspoon salt
2 eggs
¼ cup (½ stick) butter, melted
½ cup sour cream
½ teaspoon almond extract
¾ cup sliced almonds, divided
½ cup whole cranberry sauce

- Combine flour, sugar, baking powder, baking soda and salt and set aside.
- Whisk eggs, butter, sour cream and almond extract and stir in ½ cup almonds.
- Pour egg mixture into flour mixture and blend just until moist.
- Spoon batter into greased muffin pan. (Place 2 tablespoons batter into each cup.)
- Top each with 1 tablespoon cranberry sauce, evenly pour in remaining batter and sprinkle remaining almonds over top.
- Bake at 375° for 30 to 35 minutes.

Yield: 12 muffins.

Banana-Nut Muffins

½ cup (1 stick) butter, softened
1 cup sugar
2 eggs
1 cup mashed ripe bananas
½ cup chopped pecans
2 cups flour
1 teaspoon baking soda

- Mix butter, sugar, eggs, bananas, pecans, flour and baking soda in that order.
- Pour batter into greased muffin pans and fill three-fourths full.
- Bake at 350° for 15 to 20 minutes.

Yield: 24 muffins.

Easy Cheesey Muffins

3¾ cups buttermilk biscuit mix
1¼ cups grated cheddar cheese
1 egg, beaten
1¼ cups milk
Dash chili powder

- In large bowl, combine all ingredients and beat vigorously by hand.
- Pour into greased muffin tins.
- Bake at 325° for 35 minutes.

Raisin-Ginger Muffins

1 (16 ounce) box gingerbread mix
1 egg
2 (1½ ounce) boxes seedless raisins

- Combine gingerbread mix and egg with 1¼ cups lukewarm water and mix well. Stir in raisins.
- Pour into sprayed muffin tins and fill half full.
- Bake at 350° for 20 minutes or until toothpick inserted in center comes out clean.

Raisin Bran Muffins

1 (15 ounce) box Raisin Bran cereal
3 cups sugar
5 cups flour, sifted
2 teaspoons baking soda
2 teaspoons salt
4 eggs, beaten
1 cup oil
1 quart buttermilk

- Mix cereal, sugar, flour, baking soda and salt.
- Add eggs, oil and buttermilk and beat well.
- Pour batter into greased muffin pans and fill each cup two-thirds full.
- Bake at 400° for 15 to 20 minutes.

Yield: 90 muffins.

Tip: This batter may be stored in a covered container in the refrigerator for up to six weeks.

Pineapple-Bran Muffins

2 1/2 cups flour
1 1/2 cups sugar
2 1/2 teaspoons baking soda
1 teaspoon salt
1/2 teaspoon cinnamon
1/4 teaspoon allspice
2 1/2 cups bran cereal
1 (8 ounce) can crushed pineapple with juice
2 eggs, beaten
2 cups buttermilk
1/2 cup oil

- Sift together flour, sugar, baking soda, salt, cinnamon and allspice and mix in cereal.
- Combine pineapple, eggs, buttermilk and oil.
- Add pineapple mixture to flour mixture and stir just until dry ingredients are moist.
- Pour batter into greased muffin pan.
- Bake at 400° for 15 to 20 minutes.

Yield: 24 muffins.

Peach Muffins

1½ cups flour
¾ teaspoon salt
½ teaspoon baking soda
1 cup sugar
2 eggs, well beaten
½ cup oil
1¼ cups fresh or canned peaches, drained,
  coarsely chopped
½ teaspoon vanilla extract
½ teaspoon almond extract
½ cup chopped almonds

- Combine flour, salt, baking soda and sugar.
- Make hollow in center of flour mixture and add eggs and oil. Stir just until dry ingredients are moist.
- Stir in peaches, both extracts and nuts.
- Pour batter into greased muffin pan. (Place about ⅓ cup batter in each cup.)
- Bake at 350° for 20 to 25 minutes.

Yield: 12 muffins.

Miniature Cherry Muffins

4 tablespoons ($^1/_2$ stick) butter
$^1/_2$ cup sugar
$^1/_2$ cup packed brown sugar
2 eggs, separated
1 cup flour
$^1/_4$ teaspoon baking powder
1 (10 ounce) jar maraschino cherries with
  juice
$^3/_4$ cup finely ground pecans
Powdered sugar

- Cream butter and both sugars.
- Beat 2 egg yolks well and add to creamed mixture.
- Add flour, baking powder and 2 tablespoons cherry juice.
- Beat egg whites well and fold into batter.
- Grease miniature muffin pan and sprinkle pecans into each cup.
- Cover pecans with 1 teaspoon batter and place 1 cherry on top of batter in each cup.
- Top with another teaspoon batter and sprinkle with pecans.
- Bake at 400° for 10 minutes. Roll muffins in powdered sugar while still warm.

Yield: 36 muffins.

Baker Blueberry Muffins

1³/₄ cups sugar
¹/₂ cup oil
¹/₂ cup (1 stick) butter, softened
2 eggs
3¹/₄ cups flour
1 tablespoon baking powder
1 teaspoon baking soda
1 cup buttermilk
2 teaspoons butter flavoring
2 teaspoons vanilla extract
¹/₂ (15 ounce) can blueberries, drained

- Cream sugar, oil and butter.
- Add eggs and cream thoroughly.
- Combine flour, baking powder and baking soda and gradually add flour mixture to creamed mixture alternately with buttermilk. Beat well after each addition. (Begin and end with flour mixture.)
- Add butter flavoring and vanilla and fold in blueberries.
- Pour batter into greased muffin pans and fill two-thirds full.
- Bake at 350° for 20 minutes.

Yield: 24 muffins.

Butterscotch-Apple Muffins

3 cups self-rising flour
$\frac{1}{4}$ cup sugar
2 eggs, beaten
1$\frac{1}{2}$ cups milk
$\frac{1}{3}$ cup oil
1 (6 ounce) package butterscotch chips
1 cup peeled, diced apples

- Sift flour and combine with sugar.
- Add eggs, milk, oil, butterscotch chips and apples to flour mixture and stir just until moist.
- Pour batter into greased muffin pans and fill each cup two-thirds full.
- Bake at 425° for 15 to 20 minutes.

Yield: 18 large muffins or 48 small muffins.

*Tip: If you're making small muffins,
bake 10 to 12 minutes.*

Honey-Poppy Seed Muffins

1 cup flour, sifted
1 cup cornmeal
1 tablespoon baking powder
2 teaspoons poppy seeds
2 eggs, beaten
$^2/_3$ cup milk
$^2/_3$ cup honey
$^1/_4$ cup oil

- Combine flour, cornmeal, baking powder and poppy seeds.
- Combine eggs, milk, honey and oil.
- Add egg mixture to flour mixture in one addition and stir just until moist.
- Pour batter into greased muffin pan and fill each cup two-thirds full.
- Bake at 425° for 15 minutes or until brown.

Yield: 12 muffins.

Honey-Peanut Butter Muffins

1 cup whole wheat flour
1 cup all-purpose flour
1 cup chopped, salted peanuts
1 tablespoon baking powder
¼ teaspoon salt
1 cup honey
1⅓ cups evaporated milk
1 cup smooth peanut butter
1 egg

- Combine whole wheat and all-purpose flours, peanuts, baking powder and salt and set aside.
- In small mixing bowl, combine honey, evaporated milk, peanut butter and egg.
- Add honey mixture to flour mixture in one addition and stir just until moist.
- Spoon batter into lightly greased muffin pans.
- Bake at 350° for 20 to 25 minutes.

Yield: 24 muffins.

Chocolate-Oatmeal Muffins

1 cup oatmeal
1 1/2 cups boiling water
1 cup flour
1/2 cup cocoa
1 teaspoon baking soda
1/2 teaspoon salt
1/2 cup (1 stick) butter, softened
1 cup sugar
2 eggs
1 teaspoon vanilla extract
Powered sugar

- Stir oatmeal into boiling water, immediately remove from heat and set aside.
- Sift together flour, cocoa, baking soda and salt and set aside.
- Cream butter, sugar and eggs.
- Add flour mixture and oatmeal to creamed mixture, mix well and add vanilla.
- Pour batter into greased muffin pans.
- Bake at 350° for 20 minutes. Dust with powdered sugar.

Yield: 12 muffins.

Tip: You must use real butter for this recipe—
no substitutions.

Chocolate Chip Muffins

³/₄ cup milk
¹/₂ cup oil
1 egg, beaten
2 cups flour
¹/₃ cup packed brown sugar
3 teaspoons baking powder
1 teaspoon salt
1 teaspoon vanilla extract
²/₃ cup chocolate chips

- Add milk and oil to beaten egg.
- Stir in flour, brown sugar, baking powder, salt and vanilla just until moist.
- Fold in chocolate chips, pour batter into greased muffin pan and fill each cup three-fourths full.
- Bake at 400° for 25 minutes.

Yield 12 muffins.

Biscuit Muffins

2$\frac{1}{2}$ cups flour
$\frac{1}{4}$ cup sugar
1$\frac{1}{2}$ tablespoons baking powder
$\frac{3}{4}$ cup (1$\frac{1}{2}$ sticks) butter
1 cup milk

- Combine flour, sugar and baking powder.
- Cut in butter with pastry blender until mixture resembles coarse crumbs.
- Stir in milk just until mixture is moist and spoon batter into greased muffin pan.
- Bake at 400° for 18 to 20 minutes or until brown. Yield: 12 muffins.

Beer Muffins

2 cups biscuit mix
2 teaspoons sugar
$\frac{2}{3}$ cup beer
1 egg, lightly beaten

- Combine biscuit mix and sugar and add beer and egg.
- Pour batter into greased muffin pan and fill each cup two-thirds full.
- Bake at 400° for 15 minutes.

Sharp Cheese Muffins

2 tablespoons ($^1/_4$ stick) butter, divided
$^1/_2$ cup chopped onion
$1^1/_2$ cups biscuit mix
1 cup (4 ounces) shredded sharp cheese, divided
1 egg, lightly beaten
$^1/_2$ cup milk
1 tablespoon sesame seeds, toasted

- Melt 1 tablespoon butter in skillet over medium-high heat.
- Add onion to skillet and sauté until tender.
- Combine sautéed onion, biscuit mix and $^1/_2$ cup cheese.
- Stir in egg and milk just until biscuit mix is moist.
- Spoon mixture into greased muffin pan and fill each cup half full.
- Sprinkle batter evenly with remaining $^1/_2$ cup cheese and sesame seeds and dot evenly with remaining 1 tablespoon butter.
- Bake at 400° for 12 minutes.

Yield: 12 muffins.

Mayo Muffins

1¼ cups flour
3 tablespoons mayonnaise
1 cup whole milk

- Combine all ingredients and spoon into sprayed muffin tins.
- Bake at 375° for 20 minutes or until muffins are light brown.

Sour Cream Cornbread

1 cup self-rising cornmeal
1 (14 ounce) can cream-style corn
1 (8 ounce) carton sour cream
3 large eggs, lightly beaten
¼ cup oil

- Heat lightly greased 8-inch cast-iron skillet in oven at 400°.
- Combine all ingredients and stir just until moist.
- Remove prepared skillet from oven and spoon batter into hot skillet.
- Bake at 400° for 20 minutes or until golden.

Baker Banana Bread

$\frac{1}{2}$ cup (1 stick) butter, softened
$1\frac{1}{2}$ cups sugar
2 eggs, separated
3 bananas, mashed
1 teaspoon baking soda
4 tablespoons buttermilk
$1\frac{1}{2}$ cups flour
1 teaspoon vanilla extract

- Cream butter and sugar. Add egg yolks and mix until they blend.
- Add bananas.
- Dissolve baking soda in buttermilk and add to butter mixture.
- Add flour and vanilla and fold in 2 well beaten egg whites.
- Bake at 350° for 1 hour.

Strawberry Bread

¹/₂ cup sugar
¹/₂ cup (1 stick) butter, softened
1 teaspoon vanilla extract
2 eggs
2 cups flour
¹/₂ teaspoon salt
¹/₄ teaspoon baking soda
1 cup strawberry preserves
¹/₂ cup buttermilk
¹/₂ cut chopped nuts

- Cream sugar, butter and vanilla until light and fluffy.
- Add eggs to creamed mixture one at a time and beat well after each addition.
- Sift together flour, salt and baking soda and set aside.
- Combine preserves and buttermilk in small bowl and blend well.
- Add flour mixture and preserve mixture to creamed mixture and beat just until they blend.
- Stir in nuts and pour dough into greased loaf pan.
- Bake at 325° for 1 hour 30 minutes. Cool in pan for 10 minutes.

Maraschino Bread

1 (8 ounce) jar maraschino cherries with
  liquid
2 eggs
1 cup sugar
³/₄ cup chopped nuts
1¹/₂ cups flour
1¹/₂ teaspoons salt
1¹/₂ teaspoons baking powder

- Drain cherries and reserve liquid.
- Combine eggs and sugar and add nuts and cherries.
- Combine flour, salt and baking powder. Add flour mixture to egg mixture alternately with reserved cherry liquid and beat well after each addition.
- Pour dough into greased loaf pan.
- Bake at 350° for 45 minutes.

Raisin Scones

2 cups flour
2 teaspoons baking powder
$\frac{1}{2}$ teaspoon baking soda
$\frac{1}{4}$ teaspoon salt
2 tablespoons sugar
$\frac{1}{2}$ cup (1 stick) butter, softened
1 teaspoon grated lemon peel
$\frac{1}{2}$ cup raisins
$\frac{3}{4}$ cup buttermilk

- Combine flour, baking powder, baking soda, salt and sugar in mixing bowl.
- Cut in butter with pastry blender until mixture is crumbly. (The largest crumbs should be the size of small peas.)
- Add lemon peel and raisins and blend.
- Add buttermilk and stir until moist.
- Turn dough onto floured surface and knead 6 to 8 times. Divide dough in half, shape each portion into 7-inch circle and place on ungreased baking sheet.
- Cut each circle into 6 wedges, but do not separate. Brush tops with milk and sprinkle with sugar.
- Bake at 375° until golden, about 12 to 15 minutes. Transfer scones to wire rack.

Caraway-Raisin Bread

5 cups flour
1 cup sugar
1 tablespoon baking powder
$1^{1}/_{2}$ teaspoons salt
1 teaspoon baking soda
$^{1}/_{2}$ cup (1 stick) butter, softened
$2^{1}/_{2}$ cups seedless white raisins
3 tablespoons caraway seeds
$2^{1}/_{2}$ cups buttermilk
1 egg, slightly beaten

- Sift together flour, sugar, baking powder, salt and baking soda. Cut in butter until mixture is crumbly.

- Stir in raisins and caraway seeds.

- Add buttermilk and egg and stir just until all ingredients combine. (Mixture will appear lumpy.)

- Turn into well greased 11-inch heavy cast-iron skillet.

- Bake at 350° for 1 hour or until bread is firm and brown.

Herb Focaccia

1 (11 ounce) can refrigerated French bread
dough
2 tablespoons olive oil
1 teaspoon kosher salt
1 teaspoon freshly ground pepper
1 teaspoon dried oregano
1 teaspoon dried basil
$1/2$ teaspoon dried thyme

- Unroll dough into 15 x 10-inch jellyroll pan
  and flatten slightly.
- Press wooden spoon handle into dough to
  make indentations at 1-inch intervals.
- Drizzle dough with oil and sprinkle with
  salt, pepper, oregano, basil and thyme.
- Bake at 375° for 10 minutes or until light
  brown.

Texas Beer Bread

3 cups self-rising flour
¹/₄ cup sugar
1 (12 ounce) can beer
1 egg, beaten
Melted butter

- Mix flour and sugar in bowl.
- Add beer to flour mixture, stir just until it blends and pour into greased loaf pan.
- Combine egg with 1 tablespoon water and brush top of loaf with egg mixture.
- Let rise 10 minutes.
- Bake at 350° for 40 to 45 minutes.
- Brush top with butter.

Olive Bread

2$^1/_4$ cups flour
4 teaspoons baking powder
$^3/_4$ cup sliced pimento-stuffed olives
$^1/_4$ cup sugar
1 egg, beaten
1$^1/_4$ cup milk
2 tablespoons ($^1/_4$ stick) butter, melted

- Sift together flour and baking powder and add olives and sugar.
- Combine egg, milk and butter in bowl and mix well.
- Add egg mixture to flour mixture and stir just enough to moisten flour.
- Place dough in greased loaf pan.
- Bake at 375° for 1 hour.

Vintage Parmesan Bread

2 cups biscuit mix
1 tablespoon sugar
$^1/_2$ teaspoon dried oregano
$^1/_2$ cup grated parmesan cheese, divided
$^1/_4$ cup ($^1/_2$ stick) butter, melted
$^1/_4$ cup dry white wine
1 egg, lightly beaten
$^1/_2$ cup milk

- Combine biscuit mix, sugar and oregano and stir in $^1/_4$ cup cheese.
- Add butter, wine, egg and milk and mix well.
- Spoon dough into greased 8-inch baking dish and sprinkle with remaining cheese.
- Bake at 400° for 20 to 25 minutes.

Cheese Straws

1 1/2 cups flour
1 teaspoon baking powder
1 teaspoon salt
1/4 teaspoon pepper
2 cups grated cheese
1/4 cup (1/2 stick) butter, softened

- Sift together flour, baking powder, salt and pepper in mixing bowl.
- Add cheese and mix well.
- Cut in butter until mixture is crumbly and add enough cold water to make stiff dough.
- Turn dough onto floured surface and roll to 1/4-inch thickness.
- Cut dough into strips and place on baking sheet.
- Bake at 375° until light brown, about 10 to 12 minutes.

Soft Pretzels

1 (.75 ounce) packet dry yeast
1 tablespoon sugar
2 teaspoons salt
4 cups flour
1 egg yolk
Coarse salt

- Dissolve yeast in $1\frac{1}{2}$ cups lukewarm water.
- Add sugar and salt and stir until they dissolve.
- Stir in flour until all ingredients mix well.
- Turn dough onto floured board and knead for about 5 minutes.
- Roll dough into thin strips and shape into pretzels. Place pretzels on well greased baking sheet.
- Beat egg yolk with 1 tablespoon lukewarm water and brush on pretzels. Sprinkle generously with coarse salt.
- Bake at 425° for 15 to 20 minutes.

Sally Lunn Bread

2 (.75 ounce) packets dry yeast
4 eggs
1 cup warmed milk
$\frac{1}{2}$ cup (1 stick) butter, melted
3 tablespoons sugar
1 teaspoon salt
4 cups flour

- Dissolve yeast in $\frac{1}{4}$ cup warm water and let stand about 5 minutes.
- Beat eggs in large bowl until light in color.
- Add milk, butter, sugar, salt and yeast mixture to eggs. Stir in flour and knead until smooth.
- Place dough in greased bowl and cover with towel. Let rise until dough volume has doubled.
- Punch down and place in greased springform pan. Cover with towel and let rise for 1 hour 15 minutes.
- Bake at 350° for 40 minutes.

Garlic Casserole Bread

1 cup milk, scalded
3 tablespoons sugar
2 teaspoons salt
2 tablespoons (¼ stick) butter
2 (.75 ounce) packets dry yeast
½ teaspoon garlic powder
4 cups flour

- Mix milk, sugar, salt and butter in bowl. Cool to lukewarm.
- Dissolve yeast in 1 cup warm water and stir into milk mixture.
- Add garlic powder and flour and beat until ingredients blend.
- Cover and let rise in warm place for 40 minutes or until dough volume doubles.
- Stir dough down, knead for 30 minutes and turn into greased 1½-quart casserole dish.
- Bake at 375° for 1 hour.

Italian-French Bread

1 (.75 ounce) packet dry yeast
1 cup spaghetti sauce
1 tablespoon sugar
1 tablespoon grated parmesan cheese
1$\frac{1}{2}$ teaspoons garlic salt
$\frac{1}{2}$ teaspoon basil
$\frac{1}{2}$ teaspoon oregano
3 tablespoons olive oil
6$\frac{3}{4}$ to 7 cups flour

- Dissolve yeast in 1$\frac{1}{2}$ cups warm water. Stir in spaghetti sauce, sugar, cheese, garlic salt, basil, oregano and olive oil and add flour gradually to form stiff dough.

- Knead dough for 5 minutes and place in greased bowl.

- Cover and let rise in warm place for about 1 hour or until dough volume doubles.

- Divide dough into three parts and shape each part into thin loaf about 12 inches long.

- Place loaves on greased baking sheets.

- Cover and let rise in warm place for about 45 minutes or until dough volume doubles.

- Bake at 375° for 30 to 35 minutes.

Buttermilk Rolls

2 (.75 ounce) packets dry yeast
1½ cups lukewarm buttermilk
3 tablespoons sugar
¼ oil
4½ cups flour
½ teaspoon baking soda
1 teaspoon salt

- Dissolve yeast in ¼ cup warm water and add buttermilk, sugar and oil.
- Sift flour, baking soda and salt into yeast mixture. Mix well and knead 10 minutes.
- Pinch off 2-inch balls of dough and place in greased baking dish. Cover and let rise until dough volume doubles.
- Bake at 400° for 15 minutes. Brush with melted butter.

Yield: 18 rolls.

Potato Biscuits

1 (.75 ounce) packet dry yeast
2¹/₂ cups flour
1 (1.25 ounce) packet dry chicken gravy
  mix
¹/₂ cup instant mashed potato flakes
2¹/₂ tablespoons sugar
4 teaspoons baking powder
1 teaspoon salt
¹/₂ teaspoon baking soda
¹/₂ cup shortening
1 cup buttermilk
Melted butter

- Dissolve yeast in ¹/₄ cup warm water.

- Combine flour, gravy mix, potato flakes, sugar, baking powder, salt and baking soda and cut in shortening with pastry blender.

- Add yeast mixture and buttermilk and stir just until they blend.

- Knead 4 to 6 times or until dough is no longer sticky.

- Roll out or pat dough to ³/₄-inch thickness and cut into rounds with 2-inch biscuit cutter.

- Place biscuits on lightly greased baking sheet and brush tops with melted butter.

- Bake at 450° for 8 to 10 minutes.

Sweet Potato Rolls

2 (.75 ounce) packets dry yeast
3 cups whole wheat flour
3 cups all-purpose flour
$^{1}/_{3}$ cup packed brown sugar
1$^{1}/_{4}$ teaspoons salt
$^{1}/_{4}$ cup plain yogurt
4 tablespoons ($^{1}/_{2}$ stick) butter
1 egg
1 (16 ounce) can sweet potatoes, drained

- Dissolve yeast in 1$^{1}/_{2}$ cups warm water.
- Combine whole wheat and all-purpose flours.
- Add 1 cup flour mixture, brown sugar, salt, yogurt, butter, egg and sweet potatoes to yeast mixture and mix well.
- Stir yeast mixture into remaining flour mixture and knead for 5 minutes.
- Place dough in greased bowl, cover and let rise until dough volume doubles.
- Punch dough down and divide in half. Roll each half into 16-inch circle and cut each circle into 16 wedges.
- Roll up wedges and place on greased baking sheets. Cover and let rise until dough volume doubles.
- Bake at 350° for 15 minutes.

Cheesy Herb Bread

1 (16 ounce) loaf unsliced French bread
1/2 teaspoon garlic powder
1 teaspoon marjoram leaves
1 tablespoon dried parsley leaves
1/2 cup (1 stick) butter, softened
1 cup parmesan cheese

- Slice bread into 1-inch slices.
- Combine garlic, marjoram, parsley and butter. Spread mixture on bread slices and sprinkle with cheese.
- Wrap in foil and bake at 375° for 20 minutes. Unwrap and bake 5 more minutes.

Quick Pumpkin Bread

1 (16 ounce) package pound cake mix
1 cup canned pumpkin
2 eggs
1/3 cup milk
1 teaspoon allspice

- With mixer, beat all ingredients and blend well. Pour into greased, floured 9 x 5-inch loaf pan.
- Bake at 350° for 1 hour. Use toothpick to test for doneness. Cool and turn out onto cooling rack.

Sweet Milk-Yeast Bread

8 cups flour, divided
1 tablespoon sugar
1 tablespoon salt
2 (.75 ounce) packets dry yeast
1 (14 ounce) can sweetened condensed milk
$\frac{1}{3}$ cup oil
Melted butter

- Sift together 6 cups flour, sugar, salt and yeast in bowl.
- Combine sweetened condensed milk and oil with enough water to make 4 cups liquid and mix well.
- Add sweetened condensed milk mixture to flour mixture and blend well.
- Sift remaining 2 cups flour, add flour to dough and mix well. Knead 10 minutes.
- Place dough in greased bowl and turn until entire surface of dough is greased. Cover and let rise in warm place until dough volume doubles.
- Punch down, divide dough in half and place in two greased loaf pans. Cover and let rise until dough volume doubles.
- Bake at 350° for 50 minutes. Brush with melted butter.

  Yield: 2 loaves.

Sour Cream Biscuits

2 cups plus 1 tablespoon flour
3 teaspoons baking powder
$\frac{1}{2}$ teaspoon baking soda
$\frac{1}{2}$ cup shortening
1 (8 ounce) carton sour cream

- Combine flour, baking powder and baking soda, add a little salt and cut in shortening.
- Gradually add sour cream and mix lightly.
- Turn onto lightly floured board and knead a few times. Roll to $\frac{1}{2}$ -inch thickness.
- Cut with biscuit cutter and place biscuits on greased baking sheet.
- Bake at 400° for 15 minutes or until light brown.

Index

Index ~~~~~~

Index

Index ᐳᐳ

Index

COOKBOOKS PUBLISHED BY COOKBOOK RESOURCES, LLC

The Ultimate Cooking with 4 Ingredients
Easy Cooking with 5 Ingredients
The Best of Cooking with 3 Ingredients
Gourmet Cooking with 5 Ingredients
Healthy Cooking with 4 Ingredients
Diabetic Cooking with 4 Ingredients
4-Ingredient Recipes for 30-Minute Meals
Essential 3-4-5 Ingredient Recipes
The Best 1001 Short, Easy Recipes
Easy Slow-Cooker Cookbook
Essential Slow-Cooker
Quick Fixes with Cake Mixes
Casseroles to the Rescue
I Ain't On No Diet Cookbook
Kitchen Keepsakes/More Kitchen Keepsakes
Old-Fashioned Cookies
Grandmother's Cookies
Mother's Recipes
Recipe Keepsakes
Cookie Dough Secrets
Gifts for the Cookie Jar
All New Gifts for the Cookie Jar
Gifts in a Pickle Jar
Muffins In A Jar
Brownies In A Jar
Cookie Jar Magic
Quilters' Cooking Companion
Miss Sadie's Southern Cooking
Classic Tex-Mex and Texas Cooking
Classic Southwest Cooking
The Great Canadian Cookbook
The Best of Lone Star Legacy Cookbook
Cookbook 25 Years
Pass the Plate
Texas Longhorn Cookbook
Trophy Hunters' Guide To Cooking
Mealtimes and Memories
Holiday Recipes
Homecoming
Little Taste of Texas
Little Taste of Texas II
Texas Peppers
Southwest Sizzler
Southwest Olé
Class Treats
Leaving Home
Easy Desserts
Bake Sale Best Sellers

To Order: **Bake Sale Bestsellers**

Please send_____ paperback copies @ $9.95 (U.S.) each $ _____

Texas residents add sales tax @ $1.34 each $ _____

 Plus postage/handling @ $6.00 (1st copy) $ _____

$1.00 (each additional copy) $ _____

Check or Credit Card (Canada-credit card only)   Total $ _____

Charge to: ☐ MasterCard   or   ☐ VISA

Account # _____

Expiration Date _____

Signature_____

Name _____

Address_____

City_____   State _____ Zip _____

Telephone (Day)_____(Evening)_____

Mail or Call:
Cookbook Resources
541 Doubletree Dr.
Highland Village, Texas 75077
Toll Free (866) 229-2665
(972) 317-6404 Fax

- -

To Order: **Bake Sale Bestsellers**

Please send_____ paperback copies @ $9.95 (U.S.) each $ _____

Texas residents add sales tax @ $1.34 each $ _____

 Plus postage/handling @ $6.00 (1st copy) $ _____

$1.00 (each additional copy) $ _____

Check or Credit Card (Canada-credit card only)   Total $ _____

Charge to: ☐ MasterCard   or   ☐ VISA

Account # _____

Expiration Date _____

Signature_____

Name _____

Address_____

City_____   State _____ Zip _____

Telephone (Day)_____(Evening)_____

Mail or Call:
Cookbook Resources
541 Doubletree Dr.
Highland Village, Texas 75077
Toll Free (866) 229-2665
(972) 317-6404 Fax